EASTER DAWN

THE 1916 RISING

TURTLE BUNBURY

SUPPORTED BY

FOUNDED IN 1828
GLASNEVIN TRUST
DARDISTOWN   GLASNEVIN   GOLDENBRIDGE

MERCIER PRESS
IRISH PUBLISHER – IRISH STORY

MERCIER PRESS

Cork

www.mercierpress.ie

© Turtle Bunbury, 2015

ISBN: 978 1 78117 258 2

10 9 8 7 6 5 4 3 2 1

A CIP record for this title is available from the British Library

Printed and bound in Dubai.

DEDICATION

To the memory of all who lost loved ones during the
Easter Rising of 1916.

Audi alteram partem.

CONTENTS

ABBREVIATIONS

AOH	Ancient Order of Hibernians
BMH	Bureau of Military History
DATI	Department of Agriculture and Technical Instruction
DORA	Defence of the Realm Act
GAA	Gaelic Athletic Association
GPO	General Post Office
IAA	Irish American Alliance
ICA	Irish Citizen Army
IPP	Irish Parliamentary Party
IRA	Irish Republican Army
IRB	Irish Republican Brotherhood
ITGWU	Irish Transport and General Workers' Union
IWFL	Irish Women's Franchise League
IWWU	Irish Women Workers' Union
NCO	Non-Commissioned Officer
OTC	Officer Training Corps
PAC	Peruvian Amazon Company
PRONI	Public Record Office of Northern Ireland
RDS	Royal Dublin Society
RIC	Royal Irish Constabulary
UCD	University College Dublin
UVF	Ulster Volunteer Force
VTC	Volunteer Training Corps
WS	Witness Statement

ACKNOWLEDGEMENTS

I am hugely indebted to Brian Kirby, MA, Ph.D., Provincial Archivist at the Irish Capuchin Provincial Archives, for providing many of the photographs for this book. I also offer my sincere thanks to Kieran O'Boyle and Anna O'Byrne of James Adams Auctioneers and to Rosemary King, the archivist at the Allen Library (North Richmond Street, Dublin), who so generously took the time to source photographs from their own archives. Thanks also to the to the National Archives of Ireland and to its Director.

This book would not have been possible without the invaluable assistance of Sarah Perrem in gathering up the photographs on these pages, ensuring each one was of a suitably high resolution and making sure all the permission boxes were ticked. I also extend my thanks to Dominic Perrem, Mary Feehan and Sharon O'Donovan for setting this project in motion.

I called upon the wise counsel of many people while researching this book, and I would like to offer special thanks to Jennifer Armstrong, Eoin Bairéad, Eddie Barrett, Ray Bateson, Ally Bunbury, Ibar Carty, Lorcan Collins, Paul Downes, Johnny Doyle, Joe Duffy, Donal Fallon, Las Fallon, Stephen Ferguson, Ray Halpin, Jim Connolly Heron, Evelyn Hughes, Kevin Keogh, Shay Kinsella, Conor Kostick, Michael Laffan, Fiona Lewis, Helen Litton, Éamon Martin, Jason McElligott, George Millar, Angus Mitchell, Bob Montgomery, Éamonn Murphy, the Estate of T. W. Murphy, Steve 'Mad Paddy' Murtagh, Paul O'Brien, John O'Callaghan, Mick O'Farrell, Pádraig Óg Ó Ruairc, Pat Quigley, Meda Ryan, Pauline Scarborough, Tom Sykes and Pádraig Yeates.

My thanks also to my genealogical colleague John Grenham for translating the 1911 census return for Seaghán Mac Diarmada (aka Seán Mac Diarmada).

The following have also helped me either directly or by providing answers to questions posed on my Wistorical page on Facebook. Many thanks to one and all: Gary Acheson, Emma Allen, Betty Ashe, Niall Bergin, Brendan Berry, Shane Bisgood, Alice Boyle, Terrance Breen, Helen Byrne, Tom Carew, Pamela Cassidy, Carainn Childers, Paul Clerkin, Sean Coghlan, SJ, Dr Marie Coleman, Sile Coleman, Alastair H. B. Butler Crampton, Brian Crowley, Ros Dee, Betty Dempsey, Noel Donnellon, Gráinne Doran, John Dorney, Valerie Dowling, Martin Doyle, Matt Doyle, Sé Merry Doyle, Myles Dungan, Patrick Dunphy, East Wall History Group, Éamonn P. Egan, Belinda Evangelista, Rory Everard, Terry Fagan, David Farrell, Keith Farrell, Will Fennell, Alex Findlater, Diarmaid Fleming, Jonathan Foley, Jordan Goodman, Brian Hanley, Sandra Heise, Jim Herlihy, Kieran Hoare, Paul Horan, Victoria House, Brian Hughes, Mark Humphrys, Arthur Johnson, Lar Joye, Martin Kelly, Shane Kenna, Dr Máire Kennedy, Rosaleen Kenny, Patrick Kirwan, Aidan Lambert, Philip Lecane, Cormac Lowth, Elmo Mac, Niall McAuley, Gerard McCarthy, Ciarán McManus, Marc McMenamin, Gregori Meakin, Fonsie Mealy, George Mealy, Gillean Robertson Miller, Joe Mooney, Maeve Murphy, Kevin Myers, Isabella Rose Nolan, Joe Nolan, Maribeth Nolan, Tarlách Ó Braoin, Ronan Ó Domhnaill, Liam Ó Duibhir, James O'Halloran, Jane O'Keeffe, Lochlann Ó Mearáin, Colin O'Reilly, Niall Smiley Oman, John Onions, Harold Peacock, Dominic Power, Helen Priestley, Michael Purcell, Charlie Raben, Breda Reynolds Raftery, Timothy Rearden, Stan Ridgeway, Peter Robinson, David Ryan, Jessica Slingsby, John Stephenson, Tom Sykes, Pádraig Turley, Jason Walsh-McLean, Noel Watson, Gerard Whelan, Des White, Trevor White, Daniel Williams, Lesley Wylie and Adrian Wynne-Morgan.

'EASTER WEEK'

by Joyce Kilmer (1886–1918)

'Romantic Ireland's dead and gone,
    It's with O'Leary in the grave.'
Then, Yeats, what gave that Easter dawn
    A hue so radiantly brave?

There was a rain of blood that day,
    Red rain in gay blue April weather.
It blessed the earth till it gave birth
    To valour thick as blooms of heather.

Romantic Ireland never dies!
    O'Leary lies in fertile ground,
And songs and spears throughout the years
    Rise up where patriot graves are found.

Immortal patriots newly dead
    And ye that bled in bygone years,
What banners rise before your eyes?
    What is the tune that greets your ears?

The young Republic's banners smile
    For many a mile where troops convene.
O'Connell street is loudly sweet
    With strains of Wearing of the Green.

The soil of Ireland throbs and glows
    With life that knows the hour is here
To strike again like Irishmen
    For that which Irishmen hold dear.

Lord Edward leaves his resting place
    And Sarsfield's face is glad and fierce.
See Emmet leap from troubled sleep
    To grasp the hand of Padraic Pearse!

There is no rope can strangle song
    And not for long death takes his toll.
No prison bars can dim the stars
    Nor quicklime eat the living soul.

Romantic Ireland is not old.
    For years untold her youth shall shine.
Her heart is fed on Heavenly bread,
    The blood of martyrs is her wine.

The Record
of the
Irish
Rebellion
of 1916.

Published By IRISH LIFE.

INTRODUCTION

About 500 metres from the old Pearse family home on present-day Pearse Street stands the two-storey red-brick St Andrew's National School. It opened in 1897 to provide primary education for 1,200 Catholic children from Dublin's Docklands. Nearly twenty years later, in 1916, eight boys from the school – scouts for the paramilitary Fianna Éireann – carried messages and firearms to rebel strongholds across Dublin in what the school's roll books for April 1916 described as 'The Poets' Rebellion'.

Many of those who sought to establish an Irish Republic in 1916 were poets, including four of the seven signatories to the Proclamation of the Republic (Patrick Pearse, Joe Plunkett, James Connolly and Thomas MacDonagh), while a fifth, Seán Mac Diarmada, enjoyed reeling off Robbie Burns' poems as his party piece. The Cork nationalist Thomas Kent, who was one of the sixteen men executed in the wake of the Rising, likewise dabbled in poetry.

Others preferred prose. Eoin MacNeill, Chief of Staff of the Irish Volunteers, was a history professor at University College Dublin. Michael O'Hanrahan was an acclaimed novelist, and, while he was not involved in the Rising itself, Erskine Childers, the man who skippered so many German guns into Ireland for the Irish Volunteers, was considered the foremost spy novelist of his generation. Roger Casement earned a knighthood for his stirring reports on the evilness of the rubber barons in the Congo and the Amazon. Arthur Griffith, the founder of Sinn Féin, was a journalist. The playwright Sean O'Casey, a past secretary of the Irish Citizen Army, was briefly interned as a possible rebel during the Rising and knew many of the players involved so well that he would immortalise them a decade later in *The Plough and the Stars*. George Bernard Shaw viewed the Rising from afar but campaigned vociferously against the executions, particularly for Casement.

Thomas MacDonagh, Constance Markievicz, the Pearse brothers and Seán Connolly had all trod the boards of the Abbey Theatre. Bulmer Hobson would later play an important role in founding the Gate Theatre. The future Hollywood actors Arthur 'Boss' Shields and John Loder served on opposing sides during the Rising, Shields with the Irish Volunteers, Loder as aide-de-camp to his father, the British General Lowe. Both men would later co-star in John Ford's 1941 drama *How Green Was My Valley*. Sara Allgood, who was nominated for an Oscar for her role as Loder's mother in the same film, was an early member of the Inghinidhe na hÉireann (Daughters of Erin) organisation set up by Maud Gonne.

Music was also of pivotal importance to many. Éamonn Ceannt once played the uilleann pipes for the Pope, Michael Mallin was an extremely talented flautist, both Thomas Ashe and Sean O'Casey founded pipe bands, and Ned Daly was a fine baritone. Denis McCullough, president of the Irish Republican Brotherhood (IRB) at the time of the Rising, was a piano-tuner who specialised in the manufacture of musical instruments. Patrick McCartan, another leading IRB man and occasional actor, became father-in-law to Ronnie Drew of The Dubliners.

Poets, actors, writers and musicians may seem an unlikely collection to lead a revolution, but their creative intellectualism echoed that of their spiritual forebears, the nationalists of the 1840s, the Young Ireland rebels, the Fenians and the founding fathers of the IRB. Indeed, Tom Clarke, who was old enough to have participated in the Fenian dynamite campaign of the early 1880s, was an intimate acquaintance of many of those who participated in the 1867 Rising and who founded the IRB. Major John MacBride, who was executed for his part in the 1916 Rising, had similarly befriended the 1848 veteran John O'Leary.

Compiled by the "*Weekly Irish Times*," Dublin.

SINN FEIN REBELLION HANDBOOK.

Easter, 1916.

A Complete and Connected Narrative of the Rising, with Detailed
Accounts of the Fighting at All Points in Dublin
and in the Country.

Story of the Great Fires, with List of Premises Involved.

Military Despatches and Official Statements.

Interesting Portraits.

Rebel Proclamations and Manifestoes.

Punishment of Rebels—Full Record of Sentences.

Casualties—Military, Royal Irish Constabulary, Dublin Metropolitan
Police, Volunteer Training Corps.

Names of Persons Interred in Glasnevin, Dean's Grange,
and Mount Jerome Cemeteries.

Official Lists of Prisoners Deported and Released.

Reports of all Public Courts-martial.

Report and Evidence of the Hardinge Commission.

Casement Trial and Sentence.

Work of the Hospitals—St. John Ambulance—City and County of
Dublin Red Cross Societies—Lists of Names.

Who's Who in the Handbook.

Et cetera.

PRICE—SIXPENCE NET
POSTAGE—HOME AND FOREIGN, THREEPENCE.

13

John O'Leary and John Mac Bride Fontenoy 1905.

In 1849 eighteen-year-old John O'Leary tried to spring the Young Ireland rebel leaders from prison. He later became one of the most powerful members of the IRB. O'Leary was immortalised by W. B. Yeats with a line in the poem 'September 1913': 'Romantic Ireland's dead and gone, / It's with O'Leary in the grave'. O'Leary was photographed in 1905, two years before his death, in a railway carriage in Belgium. He had just organised an 'Irish Pilgrimage' to Fontenoy in Belgium to commemorate the Irish Brigade who served in the French Army during the Battle of Fontenoy in 1745. Seated beside him is Major John MacBride, husband of Maud Gonne and one of the sixteen men executed in the wake of the Rising. MacBride was also to earn a few words from Yeats, who referred to him as 'a drunken, vainglorious lout' in his poem 'Easter, 1916'.

It was not just thespians and wordsmiths who led the rebels. Many were experienced soldiers. James Connolly, Michael Mallin, Kit Poole, Jack White, Bob Monteith and W. J. Brennan-Whitmore were all veterans of the British Army. Major MacBride had commanded the Irish Transvaal Brigade against the British during the Anglo-Boer War. For others, soldiering was in the blood. Tom Clarke's father was a bombardier in the Royal Artillery. Liam Mellows' father and grandfather had both been British Army officers. Hundreds of young men like Seán Heuston and Con Colbert learned how to drill with Fianna Éireann, while others such as Éamonn Ceannt and Ned Daly were simply natural-born soldiers who came into their own when the Irish Volunteers were formed.

The renaissance of the Irish republican movement in the early twentieth century owed a good deal to the northern counties. Tom Clarke spent much of his childhood in the small town of Dungannon in Co. Tyrone, as did Joe McGarrity and Patrick McCartan, two of the most influential Irish nationalists operating in the USA. Seán Mac Diarmada of Co. Leitrim was working as a tram conductor in Belfast when he first met Bulmer Hobson, a journalist from a Quaker family, with whom he began to reorganise the IRB, the main organ of Irish republicanism. In 1908 Mac Diarmada and Hobson moved to Dublin and united with Tom Clarke, lately returned from New York. Together these immensely dynamic men not only restructured the IRB but also seized control of its Supreme Council. All three were also prominent in co-founding the Irish Volunteers in November 1913, although Hobson later alienated himself from Clarke and Mac Diarmada by supporting John Redmond's takeover of the organisation. Clarke was to play a major role in the momentous funeral of Jeremiah O'Donovan Rossa, in which all the main republican bodies took part, perhaps most notably Cumann na mBan.

Eight months later the Proclamation of the Irish Republic was addressed to 'Irishmen and Irishwomen'. The inclusion of the latter in such a massive political statement was pioneering in those days before women's suffrage had

been won. Not surprisingly, women of every background joined the cause, from working-class Dubliners like Rosie Hackett and Nurse Elizabeth O'Farrell to ladies from an Ascendancy background such as Constance Markievicz and Cesca Chenevix Trench. Their contribution to the Rising was considerably muted during the decades that followed, but has been successfully reclaimed in more recent times.

1916 pictorial albums.

The Irish Republic was conceived by dreamers and poets but harnessed by the methodical minds of the IRB. When the time came for the leaders to face the firing squads, one wonders whether they anticipated that their very executions would convert the legacy of the Easter Rising from being an ill-timed failure into the catalyst that prompted a huge number of Irish people to abandon their ambivalence about Ireland's future and pin their colours to the cause of Irish nationalism. W. B. Yeats, watching from the sidelines, gasped at the effects the Rising would have on Ireland's future: 'All changed, changed utterly: / A terrible beauty is born.' It was Yeats who had mourned, 'Romantic Ireland's dead and gone, / It's with O'Leary in the grave.' And yet, as the American poet Joyce Kilmer asked, 'Then, Yeats, what gave that Easter dawn / A hue so radiantly brave?'

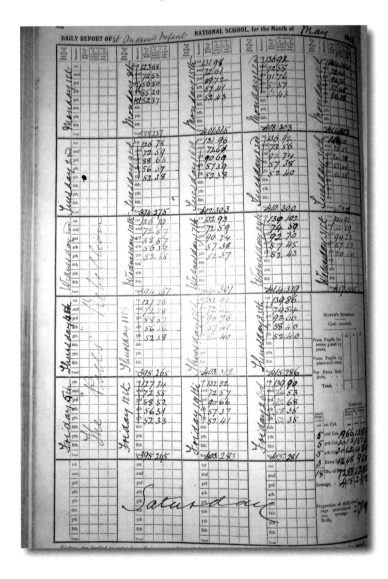

Extracts from the St Andrew's day book calling the period of the Rising 'The Poets' Rebellion'.

Joseph McGarrity

Joseph 'Joe' McGarrity was born and raised in Carrickmore, Co. Tyrone, before emigrating to Philadelphia where he became a prosperous wine and spirits merchant. He was a leading member of Clan na Gael, the most powerful of the Irish-American organisations involved in the Rising. He was also embroiled in the Hindu-German Conspiracy, a plot by radical nationalists in British India to launch a Pan-Indian rebellion against the British Raj during the First World War.[1]

Joe McGarrity became one of the principal bank-rollers of the Irish Republican Army (IRA) during the War of Independence and continued to support the organisation after it was outlawed in 1936. Shortly before his death in 1940, he is said to have met senior German officials in Berlin to request arms and funds for the IRA.[2]

Joseph McGarrity and his father, John, in their car at Dungannon, Co. Tyrone, in the early 1900s.

THE ORGANS OF
REVOLUTION

DOUGLAS HYDE

THE CULTURAL ORGANISATIONS

When it was founded in 1893 by Douglas Hyde, a Protestant academic and Irish-language scholar, the Gaelic League (Conradh na Gaeilge) was a strictly non-political organisation with a focus on the preservation of Irish language and culture. However, this was the organisation through which many of the people who would later become prominent in the republican movement first met, men such as Patrick Pearse, Eoin MacNeill and Roger Casement, as well as Éamon de Valera and most of the signatories to the Proclamation of Independence. Not surprisingly the Gaelic League became increasingly politicised and both MacNeill and Pearse served as editor of the League's newspaper, *An Claidheamh Soluis*. Hyde resigned the presidency of the League at the Dundalk Ard Fheis in 1915, when the aim of making Ireland 'free of foreign domination' was added to the articles.

An equally important cultural society which encouraged the nationalist tendencies of its members was Cumann Lúthchleas Gael, the Gaelic Athletic Association (GAA). Founded in Thurles in 1884 by a group of men with strong Fenian connections, the GAA sought to promote the Irish games of Gaelic football and hurling. More politicised than the Gaelic League, the GAA banned its members from playing what were perceived to be English games like rugby, soccer and cricket. They also barred members of the British forces, including the Royal Irish Constabulary (RIC), from joining. At least 302 members of the GAA, representing fifty-three identified Dublin clubs, participated in the Rising in Dublin. They included Harry Boland, Chairman of the Dublin County Board between 1911 and 1918, and Michael Collins, who were both in the General Post Office (GPO) during Easter Week. Many of those who fought elsewhere in Ireland during the Rising were also GAA members, such as Austin Stack, Secretary of the Kerry County Board (1904–8), and Thomas Ashe, another Kerryman, who led his battalion to victory over the RIC in Ashbourne, Co. Meath.[1] The GAA became deeply political after the Rising, and innumerable clubs adopted the names of the executed signatories to the Proclamation and others who were killed or who served at this time.

Michael Collins

Having previously worked at the Post Office in London, twenty-six-year-old Michael Collins was an important cog in the project to seize the GPO. During the week he served as aide-de-camp to the ailing Joe Plunkett. He later remarked that the rebellion 'had the air of a Greek tragedy about it'.[2] Appointed to the first IRB Supreme Council in the aftermath of the 1916 Rising, he later became perhaps the most iconic figure of Ireland's War of Independence.

THE IRISH REPUBLICAN BROTHERHOOD

The architects of the Rising, including all seven signatories to the Proclamation of Independence, were members of the IRB, a secret, oath-bound organisation whose primary objective was to establish Ireland as an 'independent democratic republic' – by armed revolution if need be. The seven signatories formed the IRB's Military Council, while five of the seven (excluding Connolly and Ceannt) were also members of the IRB's Supreme Council.

Founded at 16 Lombard Street, Dublin, on St Patrick's Day 1858, the Brotherhood was closely entwined with the Fenian Brotherhood in the USA, as well as with the Young Ireland rebels of 1848. Its structure was quasi-military: 'circles' instead of regiments, a 'centre' in place of a colonel and a series of lesser roles filled by the equivalents of captains, sergeants and rank-and-file soldiers.[3] In an attempt to prevent the organisation being infiltrated by spies, each circle was independent of the others and the members were to remain unknown to each other, although this proved easier in theory than in practice. All members swore allegiance to an Irish Republic.

Initially led by a single leader, in July 1867 a Supreme Council was established to oversee the organisation. It comprised eleven men, four of whom were co-opted, while the remainder represented the seven districts in which the IRB operated, namely the four Irish provinces, together with North England, South England and Scotland.

Supported by the Fenian Brotherhood, who launched a series of raids against various army depots and custom ports in British-controlled Canada in 1866, the IRB orchestrated the Fenian Rising of 1867 against British rule in Ireland. However, the rebellion quickly petered out and its leaders were arrested. None were executed, but the rising gained iconic status in republican lore when three IRB members – William Allen, Michael Larkin and Michael O'Brien – later known as the Manchester Martyrs, were publicly hanged in November of that year. Their crime was to have helped IRB leader Thomas Kelly and his associate Timothy Deasy escape from police custody in a raid that left one sergeant dead.

The failure of 1867 forced the IRB to change tack. For the next forty years it would seek to achieve its aims through less violent means, supporting the Home Rule campaign. The organisation also played a prominent role during the Land Wars, a campaign of civil unrest that engulfed rural Ireland during the later decades of the nineteenth century. In 1882 a radical breakaway IRB faction called the Invincibles was responsible for the assassination of Lord Frederick Cavendish, the British Chief Secretary for Ireland, and his secretary, in Dublin's Phoenix Park.

By 1905 the IRB was in danger of becoming irrelevant, having lost much of its revolutionary magnetism and sense of direction amid the meandering corridors of political power.[4] It fell to three young republicans, Denis McCullough, Bulmer Hobson and Seán Mac Diarmada, to revitalise the organisation and reassert the objective of an Irish Republic. In 1908 they received a considerable boost when John Devoy of Clan na Gael, the successor to the Fenian Brotherhood, sent the veteran Fenian Tom Clarke to oversee the reorganisation.

With Clarke at the helm, the Supreme Council was effectively purged of the old guard while the vacated seats were filled by Clarke himself (as secretary), Hobson, McCullough and Mac Diarmada.[5] By the time Patrick Pearse joined the Supreme Council in July 1914, the cast was in place for the planning of a major uprising against British rule.

Bulmer Hobson

Born in 1883, Bulmer Hobson was raised as a Quaker in Co. Down. His father had supported Gladstone's Home Rule campaign and his mother, Mary, was one of the leading lights of the Irish Women's Association in Belfast.[6] Committed to Irish nationalism by his early teens, Hobson joined both the Gaelic League and the GAA. In 1904 Denis McCullough swore the twenty-one-year-old into the IRB. Together with McCullough and Seán Mac Diarmada, Hobson became central to the reinvigoration of the IRB's appeal in Ulster, most notably through the Dungannon Clubs. In 1907 he moved to Dublin where he became a close friend of Tom Clarke, and in 1909 he co-founded Fianna Éireann with Constance Markievicz. Two years later he was part of a younger generation elevated to the Supreme Council of the IRB, becoming Chairman of the Dublin Centres Board.

In 1913 Hobson was one of the co-founders of the Irish Volunteers. He went on to play a pivotal role in organising the collection of the German rifles from the *Asgard* at Howth in 1914, after which he resigned from the Quakers on principle because his views were no longer compatible with their strict adherence to pacifism.

Hobson's star waned when he reluctantly helped John Redmond gain control of the Irish Volunteers. His actions led to a severe falling out with Clarke and he resigned from the IRB Supreme Council. He was also dismissed from his post as Irish correspondent to John Devoy's Clan na Gael newspaper, the *Gaelic American*.

Hobson was kept in the dark about the planned Easter Rising, having voiced his belief that any such rebellion would lead to the crushing of the Volunteers.[7] When he discovered the Rising was to take place on Easter Sunday, he immediately alerted MacNeill, who hastily issued his infamous countermand. Hobson was then abducted on the orders of the Rising's leaders and held at gunpoint in a safe house in Cabra until Easter Monday. He was released after the fighting had begun.

After the Rising, he took no further part in politics but he served as Chief of the Stamp Department in Dublin Castle from independence until his retirement in 1948. One of his lesser-known roles was as a major patron of the Gate Theatre in Dublin when it was founded in 1928. In later life, he lived in Roundstone, Co. Galway, and then Castleconnell, Co. Limerick, where he died in 1969, aged eighty-six.

"JOHN DALY."   "THOMAS J. CLARK."   SEAN McDERMOT."
COPYRIGHT.

The link between the rebellion leaders of 1916 and the Fenian movement of the previous century is highlighted in this photograph of Tom Clarke (*standing*) and the young Seán Mac Diarmada beside John Daly, who served with the Fenians of Limerick during the 1867 Rising. Daly, Head Centre for the IRB in Connaught, swore Clarke into the IRB in 1875. Imprisoned together during the 1880s and 1890s, the two became close friends and Clarke married Daly's niece Kathleen. This photograph is thought to have been taken in the winter of 1915, shortly after Mac Diarmada's release from prison. He had been incarcerated for giving a speech denouncing the British Army's recruitment policy in Ireland. Mac Diarmada had grown the beard while in jail.

THE IRISH CITIZEN ARMY

Established in November 1913, the Irish Citizen Army (ICA) was a citizens' militia formed to protect workers in the picket lines from attacks by the increasingly aggressive Dublin Metropolitan Police, as well as gangs in the pay of Dublin's employers. This was a direct response to a turbulent episode in Dublin's history known as the 'Lockout'. In July 1913 an Employers' Federation of some 300 Dublin-based companies had organised the lockout of over 20,000 workers who supported the Irish Transport and General Workers' Union (ITGWU) and its towering founder 'Big Jim' Larkin.

The need for such a force became particularly pertinent after 'Bloody Sunday', when police baton-charged a crowd gathered to hear Larkin speak from a balcony at the Imperial Hotel on Sackville Street (now O'Connell Street). The charge, which made international headlines, left three dead and over 500 injured; Jack White likened it to basking seals being clubbed.[8] Larkin, whose powerful oratory did so much to highlight the outrageous poverty and injustices of the time, was arrested before he could complete his speech. He was charged with breaching the peace and seditious language and sentenced to seven months in prison. Following a high-profile campaign led by George Bernard Shaw, Keir Hardie and Sylvia Pankhurst, he was released after four weeks.

The specifics about who actually conceived of the ICA are open to question. James Connolly, the deputy leader of the ITGWU, claimed it was his idea but conceded that he was fortunate to have the assistance of

DUBLIN RIOTS

ARREST
OF
JIM LARKIN

Jim Larkin
Delia Larkin

IMPER

Captain Jack White as his drilling instructor. However, White, who adored Connolly, appears to have felt it was his brainchild.[9]

Jack White, the first commandant of the ICA, was an extraordinary man. The scion of a Protestant family from Co. Antrim, he was the son of a Victoria Cross-winning field marshal and former governor of Gibraltar. As a decorated Anglo-Boer War veteran, White had served as his father's aide-de-camp in Gibraltar, but he subsequently became disillusioned with the Establishment and by 1913 was firmly in the socialist camp.

The ICA was headquartered in the ITGWU building at Liberty Hall, with branches in Tralee and Killarney in Co. Kerry. It also included the Women's Section, which was primarily assigned to provide catering and first aid for the men, as well as running the shop in Liberty Hall. Among its best-known female members were Constance Markievicz, Nellie Gifford, Madeleine Ffrench-Mullen, Kathleen Lynn and Rosie Hackett.[10]

Although the ICA was never called into action during 1913, the militia did not disband when the ITGWU was effectively defeated after a six-month stand-off. The ICA's provisional Army Council was first elected on 22 March 1914, comprising White as the first commandant and the pacifist Francis Sheehy-Skeffington as vice-chairman.[11] Sean O'Casey was elected secretary and the role of treasurer was split between Constance Markievicz and Richard Brannigan. O'Casey penned a new constitution, stating the ICA's manifest belief that 'the ownership of Ireland, moral and material, is vested of right in the people of Ireland', with a useful catch-all policy to 'sink all difference of birth, property and creed under the common name of the Irish people'.[12]

Barely a month later, White resigned from the ICA, probably because of personal differences with the mercurial Jim Larkin, especially when the latter publicly lambasted White's father as a man who had served under 'the dirty flag under which [so much] disease and degradation had been experienced'.[13] There was also an irksome incident at Butt Bridge when White and four other ICA members were part of a 200-strong mob who had a scuffle with police. White and the other ICA members emerged from the brawl badly bloodied, but most of the mob fled, after which the Dublin press unfairly lampooned the ICA as 'the runaway army'. White fought his corner in the ensuing trial until legal costs compelled him to submit.

White later joined the National Volunteers, converted his two-seater Ford motorcar into an ambulance and set off for Belgium to assist with the war effort.[14] However, when he learned of the Easter Rising and Connolly's imprisonment in May 1916, he launched an extraordinarily ill-judged attempt to free his old comrade, travelling to the coalfields of south Wales in a bid to get the miners to strike. He was arrested and sentenced to three months for sedition on the very same day that Connolly was executed. He was sent to London's Pentonville Prison where he occupied a room just forty-five metres from the shed in which Roger Casement was hanged.[15]

After White's departure from the ICA, his role as commandant was assumed by Larkin. However, Larkin's departure for a new life in the USA in October 1914 left James Connolly in sole command. By then Connolly regarded the ICA as the means by which he would secure the creation of an Irish socialist republic. O'Casey later slated Connolly for being a 'dictator, not of an army, but of a company of little more than a hundred men'.[16]

Membership of the ICA was rarely more than 250, inclining the British authorities in Dublin to adopt a largely laissez-faire attitude towards it. Connolly's army was permitted to drill and bear arms, although there were repeated raids on Liberty Hall. The first edition of the ICA's newspaper, the *Irish Worker*, edited by Connolly, contained the masthead, 'We Serve Neither King Nor Kaiser'. Not surprisingly, the *Irish Worker* was closed down under the terms of the Defence of the Realm Act (DORA) when Connolly began urging its readers to launch an insurrection against British rule and 'to carve their own future'.[17] The newspaper was reborn as *The Worker* and later as the *Workers' Republic*, still edited by Connolly, and continued to be produced until the Rising began. Connolly also played psychological tricks with the authorities by chalking messages on a blackboard outside Liberty

Hall every Saturday, calling on the ICA to prepare for an imminent attack on Wellington Barracks or Dublin Castle.[18]

On 19 January 1916 Connolly attended a meeting with Pearse, Mac Diarmada and Plunkett, which took place at the house of IRB man John Cassidy, manager of the brickworks in Dolphin's Barn.[19] During the meeting, Connolly and the IRB leaders discussed common goals, concluding that any attempt to act alone would be folly and that their best chance of a successful rebellion would be to unite. Until then, the ICA had been a stand-alone organisation; the Irish Volunteers had even rejected a proposal that it become a unit within their organisation. Henceforth, the fate of Connolly and the ICA would be entwined with that of the IRB.

Overleaf: Armed and uniformed members of the ICA drawn up in front of the ITGWU headquarters at Liberty Hall in Dublin, beneath a banner declaring 'We Serve Neither King Nor Kaiser'. This photograph was taken in 1914, some time between Connolly's election as head of the Army Council in late October and 19 December when the banner was removed by the authorities.

Sean O'Casey

Sean O'Casey was born John Casey at 85 Dorset Street, Dublin, in 1880, the youngest of seven children in a lower-middle-class Protestant family. His father was a part-time teacher and secretary to the Irish Church Missions, a proselytising body established to convert Roman Catholics to the Church of Ireland. His mother was the daughter of a prosperous auctioneer. O'Casey was plagued from an early age with chronic trachoma, an eye disease that was common in the poorer parts of Dublin. His father died of a spinal injury when he was six years old, and, low on money, his mother moved the family to East Wall, an unequivocally working-class area and borderline slum between the Great Northern Railway (GNR) on Amiens Street and the Docklands.

In 1903 O'Casey, while working as a bricklayer's assistant with the GNR, joined both the Gaelic League and the GAA and began to use the Irish form of his name, by which he is known today. He learned the Irish language and co-founded the St Laurence O'Toole Pipe Band. He joined the IRB, became intimately involved with the ITGWU and served as the first secretary of the ICA.

O'Casey was a non-combatant during the Rising but witnessed it from his home on Mountjoy Square and was briefly interned as a suspect rebel.[20] His first full-length play, *The Shadow of a Gunman*, was performed at Dublin's Abbey Theatre in 1923. The play became immensely popular, establishing O'Casey as a true working-class hero. The following spring the Abbey produced his *Juno and the Paycock* and in 1926 came *The Plough and the Stars*, the final acts of which were set against the backdrop of the Easter Rising. In 1927 O'Casey married charismatic Irish actress Eileen Carey Reynolds, with whom he settled in England. He died, aged eighty-four, in Torquay in 1964.

THE IRISH VOLUNTEERS

On the eve of the First World War, the biggest armed force in Ireland was the Irish Volunteers, or Óglaigh na hÉireann as it was known in Irish, with nearly 180,000 members. This military organisation was founded at the Rotunda Rink in Dublin on 25 November 1913 when 4,000 eager recruits crowded into the hall while a further 3,000 gathered in the old gardens just outside. Designed as the military wing of the republican movement, its formation came in response to the Ulster Volunteer Force (UVF), which had very quickly amassed over 100,000 members when it was founded in January 1913 to preserve the Union.[21]

The IRB provided much covert support for the Irish Volunteers, dispatching skilled Brotherhood members to drill the men.[22] They refrained from any public involvement for fear that any association with the IRB would invite the suppression of the Volunteers. Instead, they found the perfect front man in Eoin MacNeill, Professor of Early Irish History at University College Dublin. A Gaelic League academic, highly regarded for his integrity, Professor MacNeill became the Irish Volunteers' Chief of Staff.

The stated objective of the Irish Volunteers was 'to secure and maintain the rights and liberties common to the whole people of Ireland'.[23] Opinions varied widely as to whether this justified armed resistance, with MacNeill believing that taking up arms would only be justified if Britain launched a repressive campaign against Irish nationalists or, following the declaration of war on Germany, if Britain attempted to impose conscription on Ireland.[24]

Irish Volunteers training in Coosan Camp on the shores of Lough Ree in Co. Westmeath, in the autumn of 1915. Among the fifteen men pictured are Terence MacSwiney (*back row, 2nd from right*), who died on hunger strike while serving as Sinn Féin lord mayor of Cork in 1920; Peter Paul Galligan (*back row, 4th from right*), who cycled all the way from Dublin to Wexford to lead the Enniscorthy rebels during the Easter Rising; and Billy Mullins (*seated on ground, 4th from right*), one of the two men who carried an ominous message to Liberty Hall on Good Friday 1916 stating that Roger Casement and Austin Stack had been arrested in Tralee.

By March 1914 the Irish Volunteers numbered 20,000. Membership shot up to 50,000 over the next two months. This rise was in part a reaction to the 'Curragh Mutiny', when British officers at the Curragh army camp in Co. Kildare threatened to resign rather than oppose the UVF, an event that showed just how strong the Ulster Unionists' influence was upon British military policy in Ireland. By June Ireland was bracing itself for a seemingly inevitable civil war between Unionists and Home Rulers. The Irish Volunteers doubled its membership that same month.

With 100,000 willing Volunteers now on the books, John Redmond, leader of the Irish Parliamentary Party (IPP), decided it was time he got involved. Founded in 1882 by the iconic nationalist leader Charles Stewart Parnell, the IPP was one of the most powerful political forces in Britain and Ireland during the decades immediately before the Rising. Redmond's long quest to bring Home Rule to Ireland appeared to be on the cusp of victory when he made his move. He demanded that twenty-five members of his party be co-opted onto the Irish Volunteers' committee.[25] If the Volunteers refused, Redmond threatened to establish a rival organisation. Considering his immense popularity, this would have greatly depleted the Volunteers' strength.

The organisation was registering in excess of 5,000 new members every week by the time the Irish Volunteers' committee voted in favour of Redmond's takeover at the end of June 1914. Of the nine members who dissented, six were IRB men, including Éamonn Ceannt, Patrick Pearse, Seán Mac Diarmada and Fianna Éireann representative Con Colbert.[26] Bulmer Hobson's support of Redmond was the source of a major falling-out with Tom Clarke, his former mentor.

The following month, Hobson, Michael Rahilly (The O'Rahilly) and the veteran British diplomat Sir Roger Casement played a prominent role in the successful gun-running expeditions of the *Asgard* and *Kelpie*. There were various motives for these gun-runs. It was essential that the Irish Volunteers obtain some parity with the rival UVF, which, funded by men such as the Guinness magnate Lord Iveagh, the writer Rudyard Kipling and the American millionaire Waldorf Astor, had armed itself so successfully at Larne nine months earlier.[27] Marching with real rifles rather than broomsticks and hurleys would also be a massive confidence-booster for the men. Hobson was by now having second thoughts about Redmond's influence; converting the Irish Volunteers into an illegally armed organisation might curtail the IPP leader's enthusiasm and thereby free them from the uncertainty of political control.

When the First World War began, Redmond urged the Irish Volunteers to help Britain defeat Germany and he led a massive recruitment drive across Ireland. Twenty-four thousand men answered his call in 1914 alone and formed what became known as the National Volunteers. However, many younger, more radical minds were unimpressed by the direction in which Redmond was taking the cause of Irish freedom, not least when the Home Rule Act of September 1914 was revealed to be a considerably watered-down version of the initial deal. A sizeable minority, who retained the name Irish Volunteers, split with Redmond and turned instead to the increasingly militant policies of the IRB.

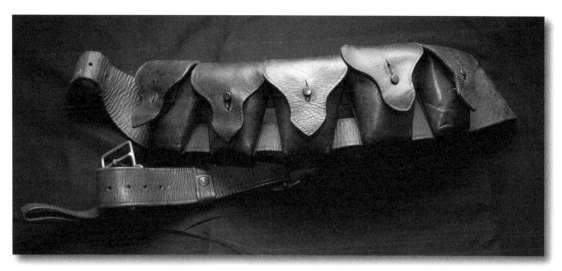

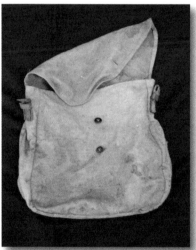

Uniform and weapons of the Irish Volunteer (*top to bottom*):

(1) A standard issue British Army P08 leather bandolier reputedly used by an Irish Volunteer during the Rising and retrieved from the gallery of the Capuchin Church of St Mary of the Angels, Dublin. The bandolier has five pouches for the storage of ammunition.

(2) A hopsack bag.

(3) Buttons from an Irish Volunteer's uniform, *c.* 1915–16.

(4) A semi-automatic pistol produced by the Savage Arms Company of Utica, New York, between 1907 and 1916. The pistol was found, along with its leather holder and a spare bullet cartridge, by a Capuchin friar on North King Street after the conclusion of the hostilities around Reilly's Fort. It has a ten-round magazine and a safety lever on the left side, at the upper rear of the grip.

Eoin MacNeill

Eoin MacNeill was born in Glenarm, Co. Antrim, in 1867. He was one of the earliest members of the Gaelic League (Conradh na Gaeilge) and was editor of its newspaper, *An Claidheamh Soluis* (*The Sword of Light*). In 1908 he was appointed Professor of Early Irish History at University College Dublin (UCD). He went on to become one of the most learned authorities on medieval Ireland.

In 1913 MacNeill published an article in *An Claidheamh Soluis* calling for the formation of a volunteer force for Irish nationalists to counter the formation of the UVF the previous year. He later chaired the council that established the Irish Volunteers and he was appointed Chief of Staff. When the organisation split in 1914,

MacNeill remained as Chief of Staff of the much reduced Irish Volunteers.

At the Gaelic League's annual Oireachtas, or cultural festival, in 1915, MacNeill led the majority of delegates who voted in favour of the organisation adopting a semi-political stance. When Douglas Hyde resigned the presidency in protest, MacNeill duly succeeded him. However, having stated his opposition to armed rebellion, MacNeill was kept out of the loop by the Rising's organisers until a few days before it was due to commence. Although he was initially persuaded to support the plans, the disastrous loss of the *Aud* and its arms compelled him to issue a countermanding order on Easter Sunday, which was probably the biggest game-changer of that tumultuous week.

After the Rising, the forty-nine-year-old professor was arrested and sentenced to life imprisonment, despite the fact that he had taken no part in the fighting. Released in 1917, he was elected as Sinn Féin MP for the National University and later for Derry city. He supported the Anglo-Irish Treaty of 1921 and was Ceann Comhairle of Dáil Éireann during the Treaty debates. He served as Minister for Education for the Irish Free State from 1922 to 1925, but lost his seat in the general election of 1927.

In later life MacNeill served as Chairman of the Irish Manuscripts Commission. He died in Dublin in 1945, aged seventy-eight.

THE WOMEN OF IRELAND

The campaign for women's suffrage in Ireland had been in motion since the 1870s. Nonetheless, women were still very much marginalised in Irish politics, excluded from the vote and from any important role in public life. Confronting this sharp imbalance became the aim of the Irish Women's Franchise League (IWFL), which was established in 1908 by Hanna Sheehy-Skeffington and her husband, Francis, along with their friends Margaret and James Cousins. However, 'suffrage before all else', the IWFL's slogan, failed to woo women like Constance Markievicz, who believed nationalism to be the predominant cause.

Those women became members of Inghinidhe na hÉireann (the Daughters of Ireland), founded in 1900 by Maud Gonne to champion the cause of anti-imperialism in Ireland during the Anglo-Boer War. The organisation attempted to temper support for Britain by organising anti-recruitment rallies and dissuading Irish women from stepping out with members of the British Army, while also promoting education for working-class children.[28] Among its early members were Helena Molony, Constance Markievicz, Kathleen Lynn and Jennie Wyse Power, all of whom participated in the Easter Rising. Others included the actress Sara Allgood, who was to be nominated for an Oscar in 1942, and her sister Molly, who was fiancée of the writer John Millington Synge at the time of his premature death in 1909.[29]

In August 1911, the women's labour movement in Ireland took a new shape in the wake of a strike at the Jacob's biscuit factory on Bishop Street. The Quaker-owned business was the largest employer of women in Dublin at the time. Although it offered one of the best working environments in the city, the men in the bakehouse went on strike, prompting 3,000 of the company's female employees to embark on a successful sympathy strike. The

Irish Women Workers' Union (IWWU) was founded on Great Brunswick Street (now Pearse Street) shortly afterwards. Jim Larkin's sister, Delia, the IWWU's first secretary, told those gathered that the women of Ireland were 'weary of being white slaves who pass their lives away toiling to fill the pockets of unscrupulous employers'.[30]

Although Eoin MacNeill had promised that there would be a role for women within the Irish Volunteers, women were not allowed to join that organisation. So, on 2 April 1914, Cumann na mBan (the League of Women) was founded at Wynn's Hotel in Abbey Street as a paramilitary auxiliary of the Volunteers. The spiritual successor of Inghinidhe na hÉireann, its primary objective was to 'advance the cause of Irish liberty and to organise Irishwomen in the furtherance of this object'. It also aimed 'to teach its members first aid, drill, signalling and rifle practice in order to aid the men of Ireland' and to 'form a fund for these purposes'.[31] Membership of the pro-suffrage Cumann na mBan came from all classes, including landed gentry such as Markievicz and future working-class icons like Rosie Hackett, although most of the women who joined were white-collar workers.

When the Volunteers split in September 1914, the vast majority of Cumann na mBan members rejected Redmond's call to enlist and maintained their role as supporters of the much-reduced Irish Volunteers.[32] By 1915 there were fifteen branches across Ireland and membership continued to rise weekly.

On the eve of the Easter Rising, the 'Army of the Irish Republic', as conceived by the IRB's Military Council, included Cumann na mBan, alongside the Irish Volunteers and the ICA.[33] The organisation played a major role in the Rising, providing many of the frontline nurses, dispatch carriers and snipers, while Jennie Wyse Power, its first president, hosted the signing of the Proclamation of the Irish Republic at her home in Henry Street.[34]

Over 200 women served with the rebels during the Rising, in every theatre of the rebellion with the exception of Boland's Mill, where the commandant, Éamon de Valera, refused to let any women serve under him, not wishing to put them in any danger.

Taken in the garden of Mr and Mrs Ely O'Carroll's house on Peter's Place, central Dublin, in the summer of 1916, this photograph shows sixty members of Cumann na mBan, Clann na nGaedheal and the ICA, each of whom served in the Easter Rising. The three women at the front are (*left to right*) Madeleine Ffrench-Mullen, Brigid Foley and Dr Kathleen Lynn. Among others in the photograph are Rosie Hackett and Nurse Elizabeth O'Farrell. The event was a meeting of the Irish National Aid Association and Volunteer Dependants' Fund.

Maud Gonne

Born in England in 1866, the actress, revolutionary and feminist
Maud Gonne claimed descent from a Catholic Irishman from Co.
Mayo who, disinherited by his father, was obliged to start anew as
a wine trader in Portugal. Her father was due to take charge of the
business but abandoned it in favour of the army, serving as an officer
in the 17th Lancers. Her mother died when she was young, and,
aside from some happy memories of living with her father at the
Curragh Camp, Co. Kildare, and in Howth, north Dublin, during

her early childhood, Maud and her sisters were largely raised by governesses in England and France. In 1885 the tall, bronze-haired beauty was presented at Dublin Castle and danced at the ball with Prince Albert Victor, eldest son of the Prince of Wales, who failed to impress her.

Desolation came the following year when typhoid killed her father, for whom she held an intense love. At the age of twenty-one, Gonne inherited an unexpected and substantial trust fund from her late mother's estate, which gave her considerable freedom. At this time she met the young W. B. Yeats, whose muse she would become. She also embarked on a lengthy affair with Lucien Millevoye, a French journalist and future politician, with whom she had a son, Georges, who died aged two in 1891, probably from meningitis. Always different, Gonne was to have sex with Millevoye in the crypt next to poor Georges' coffin in late 1893 in a bid to reincarnate her deceased son. Their daughter, Iseult, was born in August 1894.

Gonne became Queen Victoria's nemesis, organising protests against the 'Famine Queen', as she named her, during the Jubilee year of 1897 and again during Victoria's otherwise successful three-week visit to Dublin in July 1900.

When the Anglo-Boer War was at its peak in South Africa, she hosted a 'Patriotic Children's Treat', a pro-Boer fête, in Dublin on Easter Sunday 1900, attended by nearly 30,000 children. Gonne addressed the crowd, giving it her anti-imperial all, urging the children to never take a job in the British Army. That same year she founded Inghinidhe na hÉireann, the forerunner of Cumann na mBan.

Gonne's passions would perhaps never be better harnessed than in her performance as Cathleen Ní Houlihan in the play of that name written by Yeats and Lady Gregory; she stunned audiences with her portrayal of the 'old woman of Ireland', who mourns for her four provinces, unjustly seized by English colonisers. In her late thirties she converted to Catholicism, and, having repeatedly turned down Yeats' offer of marriage, she was married in Paris in 1903 to the Mayo-born Major John MacBride, a man who fought for the Boers in South Africa. Their son, Seán MacBride, winner of the Nobel Peace Prize in 1974, was born in 1904, shortly before Maud and the major separated. Maud lived in Paris for the next decade, largely so she would not have to face her husband, and served as a nurse in French military hospitals during the early years of the First World War.[35] She did not go back to Ireland until after MacBride was executed for his role in the Easter Rising.[36]

Returning to Dublin in 1918, she worked with the Irish White Cross during the War of Independence, and, like many republican women, took the anti-Treaty side during the Civil War. She died in Clonskeagh in 1958 at the age of eighty-six and is buried in Glasnevin Cemetery, Dublin. Her last recorded words were, 'I feel now an ineffable joy.'[37]

NA FIANNA ÉIREANN

The Boy Scout movement was founded by the British general Lord Baden-Powell, a hero of the Anglo-Boer War, in 1907. Two years later, Patrick Pearse apparently turned down a request by Baden-Powell to set up an Irish branch of the Boy Scouts.[38] In a further dent to Baden-Powell's pride, the Irish National Boy Scouts was established as an entirely separate entity to his organisation. Na Fianna Éireann, meaning 'Warriors of Ireland', dated its creation to a meeting of 16 August 1909, which took place in a small theatrical hall at 34 Lower Camden Street, Dublin. Among those present were Constance Markievicz, Helena Molony, Seán McGarry (a future IRB president) and Bulmer Hobson.

Markievicz had set the scouting concept in motion earlier that year when, following an introduction by Tom Clarke, she convinced McGarry to accompany her on a visit to St Andrew's National School on Great Brunswick Street (now Pearse Street) on the south side of Dublin city. They persuaded schoolteacher William O'Neill to send eight or nine St Andrew's boys to Markievicz's home in Rathgar, south Dublin, to learn about scouting. Markievicz christened them 'The Red Branch Knights'. The organisation didn't get off to a great start. As Marnie Hay put it, Markievicz 'tried – unsuccessfully – to instruct them in signalling, drill and scouting, while they – successfully – raided her husband's whiskey supply'.[39] After a muddled camping trip, she decided the organisation would require more official direction.

At this point she teamed up with Bulmer Hobson, who had attempted something similar six years earlier when he founded Fianna Éireann, a hurling league for boys and girls, in west Belfast. Hobson's outfit had failed through lack of funding, but, with Markievicz as patron, Fianna Éireann was reborn. It was billed as a national, non-party organisation, open to all Irish boys from the ages of eight to eighteen. Hobson was initially elected president but, following his return to Belfast shortly afterwards, Markievicz was elected in his place.[40]

Estimates as to how many boys showed up at the Camden Street hall that first night vary extravagantly from thirty to one hundred. Under the tutelage of young men such as Pádraig Ó Riain and Con Colbert, the boys were instructed in the military arts of drilling, signalling and scouting, as well as learning how to operate radios and shoot rifles, with a firing range in the basement.

Fianna Éireann was the first nationalist organisation in twentieth-century Ireland to begin drilling. The numbers within its ranks ebbed and flowed in the early years, but by 1912 there were twenty-two branches across Ireland, 'all in a very healthy condition'.[41] There was also a girls' branch in Belfast called the Betsy Gray sluagh, after a heroine of the 1798 rebellion, in which James Connolly's daughters Nora and Ina were leading members. This later became an important recruiting ground for Cumann na mBan.

Na Fianna Éireann's instructional handbook was first published in 1913 and included articles by Patrick Pearse and Roger Casement, another patron of the movement. By 1913 the organisation had been all but taken over by the IRB, prompting the Unionist Association of Ireland to express grave concerns about this 'Irish nursery of sedition and disloyalty'.[42] Nearly every senior Fianna officer was an IRB member, and, while Madame Markievicz, as she liked to be called, remained its president, she had little control over the direction her boys were now taking. According to Éamon Martin, 'she really had no voice in shaping policy and was overruled or outvoted whenever her ideas ran counter to the decisions of this group'.[43] Madame's power was further reduced in 1914 when the Fianna relocated their base from Surrey House, her stronghold on Leinster Road, Rathmines, to more formal premises at 12 D'Olier Street in the city centre.

When the Irish Volunteers were formed in 1913, five senior Fianna members were appointed to its provisional committee. Large numbers of Fianna scouts made a natural progression to the new organisation. When Erskine Childers sailed his yacht *Asgard* into Howth with a cargo of German rifles on 26 July 1914, 200 scouts were ready to greet him; it was they who pushed the trek cart that carried the ammunition.[44] Likewise, the Fianna were waiting in Kilcoole, Co. Wicklow, when the yacht *Kelpie* arrived with her shipment of arms five days later.

Fianna numbers dipped with the outbreak of the First World War, but steadied again by 1915. The organisation also had to contend with a growing rift between Markievicz and Hobson over the impact of the IRB takeover.

Seven Fianna were killed in action over Easter 1916, and Seán Heuston and Con Colbert, both senior Fianna officers, were executed in the aftermath.[45] The Fianna quickly reformed after the Rising, and, by June 1917, it reached an all-time high of over 30,000 members.[46]

Constance Markievicz (*seated centre front*) along with over 100 Fianna Éireann scouts at their annual ard fheis (congress) in Dublin's Mansion House in 1915. Among others in this photograph are Éamon Martin, Paddy Holohan, Barney Mellows, Garry Holohan, Bulmer Hobson and Seán Heuston, later executed for his part in the Rising, who is seated fourth from right in the second row.

Constance Markievicz

Constance Markievicz pictured at an Inghinidhe na hÉireann meeting sometime after she joined the organisation in 1909.

Constance Markievicz, eldest daughter of the Anglo-Irish land-owner and Arctic explorer Sir Henry Gore-Booth, was born at Buckingham Gate, London, in the winter of 1868. Raised on the family estate of Lissadell in north Co. Sligo, she was eleven years old when she witnessed large numbers of her fathers' tenants assemble at the house for free food when the failure of the Irish harvest prompted widespread fears of a major famine. She attributed her subsequent empathy for the working class to this moment, although such sentiments were dramatically hardened by her experiences during the 1913 Lockout.

One of her closest childhood friends was the poet W. B. Yeats, who penned a poem, 'In Memory of Eva Gore-Booth and Con Markievicz', describing the sisters as 'two girls in silk kimonos, both / Beautiful, one a gazelle'. Constance, the gazelle, went on to study at the Slade School of Art in London and at the celebrated Académie Julian in Paris.

In 1899 she met Casimir Dunin Markievicz, a large, handsome, heavy-drinking Polish artist whose family owned substantial lands near Kiev in present-day Ukraine. He claimed to be a count, although there are considerable doubts as to whether he was a bona-fide aristocrat.[47] When his wife died later that year, Constance and Casimir became close. They were married in London in 1900, and their only child, Maeve, was born the following year.

By 1903 the Markieviczes were living in Rathgar, south Dublin, mixing with the city's artistic and literary elite. Constance helped found the United Arts Club. Always drawn towards revolutionary souls, the tall, graceful brunette became friendly with Maud Gonne. She made her debut appearance at an Inghinidhe na hÉireann event by arriving at their headquarters on North Great George's Street in a satin ball-gown and diamond tiara; she had come straight from a ball at Dublin Castle.

Although initially shunned by Inghinidhe members on account of her upper-class background, she soon gained acceptance and wrote the gardening column for their monthly magazine, *Bean na hÉireann*. Her achievements before the First World War were remarkable. She co-founded Fianna Éireann, became treasurer of the ICA and designed their uniform, and became a major patron of the Liberty Hall soup kitchen during the Lockout of 1913. The following year she played an instrumental role in merging Inghinidhe na hÉireann with Cumann na mBan.

Although referred to by some as 'The Mad Countess' and 'The Loony', she was nonetheless deeply committed to the republican cause and became arguably the best-known woman of the Rising, not least because she sported a handsome feathered hat during the week, along with her top boots and service tunic. It is to be noted that the chain-smoking radical once offered her fans these unusual fashion tips: 'Dress suitably in short skirts and strong boots, leave your jewels in the bank and buy a revolver.'[48]

Having sidestepped execution after the Rising on account of her gender, she was incarcerated in Kilmainham, Mountjoy and Aylesbury prisons. In 1917 she was received into the Catholic faith and became president of Cumann na mBan, an office she held for the next seven years. At the general election in 1918, she was one of the seventy-three Sinn Féin MPs returned when that party swept the polls; she thus holds the distinction of being the first woman elected to the British House of Commons although, in line with Sinn Féin policy, she never took her seat. As Minister for Labour of the Irish Republic (1919–22), she was the second woman to become a government minister in Europe and the only one in Ireland until 1979, when Máire Geoghegan-Quinn was appointed Minister for the Gaeltacht.

Staunchly republican, her campaign to secure the release of republican prisoners set her at odds with the Free State and she was sent back to prison in November 1923. She went on hunger strike but was ordered off by the IRA after three days. She was interned in the North Dublin Union and released on Christmas

Eve 1923. When Fianna Fáil was founded, three years later, she chaired its inaugural meeting, and in June 1927 she was re-elected to the Fifth Dáil for Dublin South. However, less than five weeks later, the fifty-nine-year-old was dead, the victim of appendicitis complications. Among those at her side when she died at Sir Patrick Dun's Hospital on Grand Canal Street were Casimir and his son, Stanislas, as well as Kathleen Lynn and Hanna Sheehy-Skeffington. Éamon de Valera arrived shortly afterwards.[49] She was buried at Glasnevin Cemetery, Dublin, with de Valera giving the funeral oration. Her controversial legacy is perhaps best summed up by a remark in a letter she wrote to her brother in late 1916: 'My enemies will make a monster out of me, my friends a heroine and both are equally wide of the truth.'[50]

THE HIBERNIAN RIFLES

Based on Dublin's north side, the Hibernian Rifles were a nationalist Roman Catholic militia created in 1913. The organisation was an off-shoot of the Ancient Order of Hibernians (AOH), a Roman Catholic political association founded by Irish immigrants in New York in 1836. It was particularly close to the Irish American Alliance (IAA), the AOH's radical wing, as well as Clan na Gael.

In 1912 or 1913 the IAA dispatched John J. Scollan from Derry to oversee its three Dublin branches, namely 'The Red Hand' division in Great Brunswick Street, the 'Clan na Gael' division in Parliament Street and the 'O'Connell' division in Rathfarnham. Members became friendly with James Connolly and the ICA during the 1913 Lockout. In 1915 Scollan financed a trip by Connolly's daughter Nora to inform the German ambassador in the USA of a covert Royal Navy operation in Belfast where British arms carriers were being camouflaged as neutral civilian ships.[51]

In November 1913 Scollan initiated a recruitment drive that raised a company of twenty men from each of the IAA's Dublin divisions. These companies formed the Hibernian Rifles. Commandant Scollan was their commander-in-chief, while Cork-born John J. Walsh became vice-commandant. The men were instructed by sympathetic ex-British Army men but had no actual uniform; the lack of uniforms led to several of the first members transferring to the Irish Volunteers and the ICA.[52]

Nonetheless, by the start of 1914 the Hibernian Rifles had units in Armagh, Belfast, Castlebar, Cork, Dingle and Dundalk, albeit small outfits whose individual membership never exceeded thirty-five.[53] Moreover, they also had guns. They purchased about 100 Lee Enfield rifles – presumably illegally – from British soldiers training at the Musketry School on Bull Island off Dollymount in 1914. They also acquired about twelve shotguns and thirty Italian rifles, and manufactured their own cartridges using lead tags from postbags as shot. Hence, while most Irish Volunteer units were obliged to train with hurleys and broom handles, the Riflemen at least had rifles to work with.

The IRB was initially wary of the Hibernian Rifles, while, before the split, the Irish Volunteers were blatantly hostile, rejecting an application to affiliate the Rifles as a unit within their own organisation. However, relations strengthened in the lead-up to Jeremiah O'Donovan Rossa's funeral in 1915 when Thomas MacDonagh persuaded the Rifles to allow him and other leading Volunteers to plan the event from their headquarters at 28 North Frederick Street, Dublin.[54] This hall was also home to the north inner-city sluagh of Fianna Éireann run by Seán Heuston, and both the Keating branch of the Gaelic League and the Clan na Gael Girl Scouts.

In June 1915 the Hibernian Rifles upped their game with the launch of a weekly newspaper called *The Hibernian*, edited by Scollan, which serialised the names of all those imprisoned, deported or served with exclusion orders under DORA below the heading, 'Ireland's Roll of Honour'. At O'Donovan Rossa's funeral, the Rifles led the divisions who lowered the American flag. For the duration of the funeral, they were placed under the command of The O'Rahilly, an executive member of the Irish Volunteers.

By the autumn of 1915 relations between the Hibernian Rifles and Irish Volunteers were increasingly cordial. Scollan and Walsh visited Eoin MacNeill at his home in Herbert Park for talks at which The O'Rahilly and Desmond FitzGerald were also present. The Rifles were nonetheless kept in the dark about the Rising, although Scollan sensed that something was up and issued orders on Easter Sunday for his Riflemen to stand on parade at midday the next day. Meanwhile, the Pearse brothers and MacDonagh held a meeting in a room at the Rifles' North Frederick Street headquarters, from which they sent couriers to deliver fresh mobilisation orders to the Volunteer companies.[55]

By the afternoon of Easter Monday, Scollan and between twenty and thirty members of the Rifles had assembled at North Frederick Street to assist the rebels. Shortly after midnight, Scollan received orders from James Connolly to proceed to the GPO, where they were placed under The O'Rahilly's command and assigned to barricade the upper floors. The following day Scollan's Riflemen and a party of Volunteers from Maynooth were sent to occupy the roof of the Royal Exchange Hotel on Parliament Street where they were to provide much needed back-up to the beleaguered City Hall garrison. From the rooftops of the Exchange they repelled an attack by a combined force of Royal Irish Fusiliers and Royal Inniskilling Fusiliers, although Edward Walsh, one of the Riflemen, was fatally wounded in the action. The Rifles then returned to the GPO but several members, including Scollan, were subsequently captured. The remaining members surrendered with the GPO garrison at Parnell Street on 29 April.

Desmond FitzGerald

Although born in London, the revolutionary imagist poet and publicist Desmond FitzGerald had strong family connections in both south Tipperary and Castleisland, Co. Kerry. In his memoir of the Rising, he claimed that Pearse and Plunkett had the Kaiser's youngest son, Joachim, in mind as a possible king of Ireland in the event that Germany won the First World War.[56] He later became a minister in the Free State government, and his youngest son, Garret, served twice as Taoiseach during the 1980s.

PREPARING FOR
REBELLION

Erskine Childers (*right*) on board his yacht *Asgard* with Gordon Shepard.

ARMING THE VOLUNTEERS:
THE HOWTH AND KILCOOLE GUN-RUNNING, 1914

•••••━━━━━━━━━━━━━━━━━━━•••••

Shortly before noon on the hot, blue-skied Sunday morning of 26 July 1914, a white sail floated out from behind Lambay Island, just north of Dublin, and began to nonchalantly make its way towards the small port of Howth. *Asgard* was on the home straight from one of the most daring gun-running missions in modern history. At its helm was Erskine Childers, the best-selling spy novelist. Over the previous three weeks, he had skippered the two-masted yacht out to meet a German tugboat in the North Sea from which he received a cargo of 900 Mauser rifles and 29,000 rounds of ammunition. The weapons were destined for the hands of the Irish Volunteers who had pledged to defend Home Rule for Ireland.

Less than a week after Childers sailed *Asgard* home, Europe was to tumble into the abyss of the First World War. It is inconceivable that *Asgard*'s mission would have succeeded under wartime circumstances. And if *Asgard* had not made it back to Ireland, then the Irish Volunteers would have had precious few guns to hand when it came to launching their bid for an Irish Republic at Easter 1916. The story of *Asgard* also highlights the enormous and often overlooked role played by many leading members of the Anglo-Irish aristocracy and landed gentry in igniting the flames of Irish independence.

Born in London in 1870, Childers was the son of an English professor

Asgard at Howth in July 1914.

of Oriental languages and his Irish wife, one of the Bartons of Glendalough in Co. Wicklow. Orphaned in his childhood, Childers was raised with his four siblings and his Barton cousins on the lush 15,000-acre Glendalough estate. His formative years were typical of his class: an English public school, Cambridge, a desk job at Westminster and enlistment in the British Army in 1899 for the Anglo-Boer War. His experiences of that war – of villages in flames, of women and children incarcerated in disease-riddled concentration camps – led him to seriously question the merits of British imperialism.

Erskine's passion had always been sailing. During his twenties, he and his brother enjoyed yachting around the rocky coastline of the North Sea, keeping an eye on Germany's ever-growing naval might. In 1903 he converted his knowledge into a best-selling thriller, *The Riddle of the Sands*, which, hailed as one of the world's first spy novels, made Childers a household name. Shortly after *The Riddle* was published, Erskine attended a dinner party in Boston, where he met Molly Osgood, the daughter of Dr Hamilton Osgood, a prominent Boston physician credited with introducing the first rabies antibodies to the USA. She was a direct descendant of one of America's oldest families – her ancestors had been on board the *Mayflower*.

Molly had fractured both hips as a child and had spent twelve years on her back. She was obliged to use two canes to support herself for the remainder of her life. Despite this disability, she shared Erskine's passion for the sea and was an accomplished helmsman. She and Childers married in 1904. Her parents commissioned the yacht *Asgard* as a wedding present. The elegant 50-foot gaff ketch was custom-built at Larvik in Norway by the designer Colin Archer, one of the world's finest naval architects, to the specifications of Childers himself. He named it *Asgard*, after the mythological home of the old Norse gods. The newly-weds then settled down to a relatively low-key life in London, with much sailing around the North Sea and the Baltic on *Asgard*.

In 1908 Erskine joined his cousin Robert Barton and their friend Horace Plunkett on a motor tour of southern Ireland. The experience convinced the cousins that colonialism was fundamentally wrong, and they became open supporters of Home Rule and, from 1913, of the Irish Volunteers.

In April 1914 the Childers learned that Sir Edward Carson's Ulster Volunteers had successfully landed a shipment of 35,000 German rifles at Larne. The British authorities had seemingly watched the whole thing unfold and had done nothing to intervene. Appalled by this sudden imbalance of strength in favour of the unionists, Erskine and Molly joined a committee of well-to-do republican sympathisers who began to look at ways of arming the Irish Volunteers in a like manner. The group met at the London home of the Meath-born historian Alice Stopford Green and included Sir Roger Casement, Lord Ashbourne, Sir Alec Lawrence, Lady

Young and G. F. Berkeley, a descendant of Bishop George Berkeley. The sum of £1,524 was raised and a plan hatched.

On 28 May 1914 Childers and the political activist Darrell Figgis negotiated the purchase of 1,500 single-shot Mauser rifles (designed in 1871 and known afterwards as Howth Mausers) and 49,000 rounds of black powder ammunition from Hamburg munitions firm Moritz Magnus der Jüngere. Although they were ostensibly bargain-basement guns, they were nonetheless reasonably efficient, as the Sherwood Foresters discovered to their cost at Mount Street Bridge over Easter 1916.

Now to get them home.

The British authorities fully anticipated such an arms shipment and were ready and waiting. However, they hadn't banked on Childers' ability to spin a web of deceit right into the heart of British intelligence. False

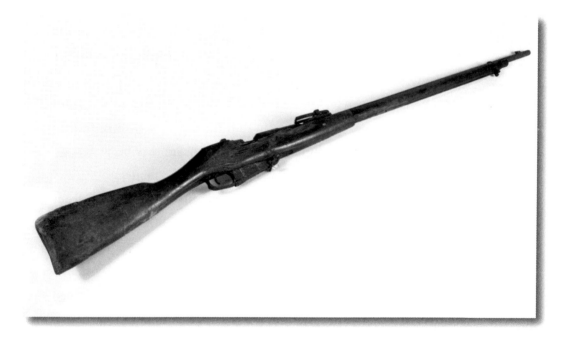

One of the Mauser Rifles which arrived in Ireland in August 1914 and was subsequently used in the 1916 Rising.

reports convinced the British that, while a shipment was en route, it was being transported by an Irish fishing trawler. And so, while the Royal Navy began intercepting all such trawlers, *Asgard* sailed out from Conwy on the Welsh coast on 3 July. On board were Erskine, Molly, Mary Spring-Rice (a cousin of the British ambassador in Washington), a British aviator and two Donegal fishermen.

Close at hand was a second yacht, *Kelpie*, a 26-ton ketch skippered by Mary Spring-Rice's Limerick cousin Conor O'Brien, and with a crew comprising his sister Kitty O'Brien, a young barrister called Diarmuid Coffey and two paid hands, Tom Fitzsimons and George Cahill. Nine days later, the two yachts rendezvoused with the German tugboat *Gladiator* just off the Belgian coast, at the Roetigen Lightship at the mouth of the Scheldt river. *Gladiator* unloaded its cargo and about-turned for Hamburg.

Kelpie was first to arrive and slipped away with the smaller part of the shipment (600 Mausers and 20,000 rounds) just as *Asgard* appeared. It took five hours for the guns and ammunition to be loaded, as the rifles had to be unpacked from canvas bases and straw before being put onto *Asgard*. The yacht was steered home through a near fatal storm, a naval review in Spithead and a brief encounter with the British warship HMS *Froward*.

On 26 July *Asgard* rolled out from behind Lambay Island, arriving into Howth harbour at 12.45 p.m. Standing in neat formation along the pier were 800 members of the Irish Volunteers and Fianna Éireann, headed up by Bulmer Hobson, The O'Rahilly and Eoin MacNeill. The party was well prepared to receive the haul. Shortly before *Asgard* hove into view, phone lines were cut and a Fianna trek cart was emptied of its 150 oak batons. Lookouts were stationed near every coastguard and police station in the vicinity. The Volunteer officers were informed that one of the reasons they had been parading their men back and forth so much over the past few weeks was so that it wouldn't look remotely suspicious when, say, a handsome two-masted yacht landed alongside them in broad daylight with a cargo of 900 Mausers and 29,000 rounds of ammunition.

When the authorities in Dublin Castle became aware of the Howth landing, they immediately dispatched a force of the Dublin Metropolitan Police to disarm the Volunteers. After a small skirmish on the Howth Road, the police secured an ineffectual haul of nineteen guns. Meanwhile, on Hobson's command, the Volunteers dissolved into the fields and by-ways; the guns and ammunition boxes vanished into thatched roofs and drainpipes, hedges and holes.

The day ended on an ominous note when, in the wake of the landing, a detachment of British soldiers from the King's Own Scottish Borderers opened fire on an angry crowd who were pelting them with rotten fruit on Bachelor's Walk, leaving three civilians dead and thirty-two wounded. One of the wounded was a boy called Luke Kelly, whose son and namesake was the celebrated singer with The Dubliners.

News of *Asgard*'s heroic landing and the 'Bachelor's Walk massacre' spread like wildfire through the country. Many feared that a full-blown war with the Ulster Volunteers was imminent, not least when the remainder of the German armaments landed at Kilcoole, Co. Wicklow, on 1 August. *Kelpie* had been relieved of its load off Wales by the engine-powered *Chotah*, skippered by Sir Thomas Myles. Hampered by a split in her main sail off the coast of Wales, *Chotah* reached the Kish Bank off the coast of Dublin on 1 August, nearly a week after the Howth landing. That evening, Eoin MacNeill dispatched a 35-foot fishing boat called the *Nugget* to meet it. The fishing boat was crewed by the McLoughlin brothers and Michael Moore, and also carried some of MacNeill's men. They successfully transferred the weapons to the *Nugget*, which took them on to Kilcoole Strand, where the consignment was landed, shortly before dawn. The greeting party included Cathal Brugha and Seán T. O'Kelly, who was destined to become president of Ireland. The *Nugget* then innocently went out for a day's fishing before returning to Howth.

Three days later, Britain declared war on Germany and the world 'slith-ered over the brink into the boiling cauldron of war', as David Lloyd George put it.[1] Childers threw himself behind the Allied cause, primarily as an observer and intelligence officer for the Royal Naval Volunteer Reserve, over the North Sea, in Gallipoli and in the Sinai Peninsula. He won the Distinguished Service Order and retired with the rank of major. However, he was so appalled by the execution of the leaders of the Easter Rebellion in 1916, and the subsequent impasse of the Irish Convention, that he followed the lead of his cousin Robert Barton and joined Sinn Féin.

He served as Director of Propaganda for the underground Dáil cabinet in 1920 as well as Chief Secretary for the delegation that negotiated the Anglo-Irish Treaty. He steadfastly opposed the Treaty itself and became one of de Valera's inner circle. In 1922 the 'damned Englishman', as Arthur Griffith now referred to him, was arrested by Free State soldiers, charged with possession of a gun and executed by a firing squad in Beggar's Bush Barracks.

Sir Thomas Myles

In 1882 a young surgeon called Tom Myles was the first doctor on the scene when Lord Frederick Cavendish, the Irish Chief Secretary, and his undersecretary were fatally attacked in Dublin's Phoenix Park. Over the next forty years, this surgeon built up an exemplary resumé: a president of the Royal College of Surgeons, an honorary burgess of Limerick city, the honorary surgeon to the King in Ireland and the recipient of a knighthood bestowed by Edward VII.

For all the royal pomp, the Limerick-born Myles, who once served as Charles Stewart Parnell's bodyguard, had been committed to Home Rule since the early days. He was also a skilled yachtsman, and, when he learned of the plan to bring German guns to Ireland in August 1914, he met with Bulmer Hobson and offered the services of his steam-yacht *Chotah*.

Myles played an important part in the Easter Rising, treating many wounded men, from both sides, in the Richmond Surgical Hospital on North Brunswick Street, which he had run since 1890.

Fianna Éireann commandant Éamon Martin, who was present at both the Kilcoole and Howth landings, recounted a meeting with Myles on Easter Monday 1916. Martin was making his way to the GPO to report on the attack on the Magazine Fort in Phoenix Park when he chanced upon Myles outside the Richmond Hospital. They reminisced briefly about their last encounter at Kilcoole before Myles declared his belief that the Rising was a mad venture.

When Martin was shot in his chest and lung the following evening, Myles had him and some twenty-five other Volunteers brought into a ward at the Richmond for treatment. After the rebels surrendered, the police maintained tight surveillance on the hospital. However, when Martin was suitably recovered, Myles engineered his escape by donning his British uniform and then escorting him away from the hospital in his chauffeur-driven car. He subsequently helped Martin get all the way to the USA. Myles remained an active sailor until his death in 1937.

THE SPLIT IN THE VOLUNTEERS

The outbreak of the First World War was to have a profound effect on both the political situation in Ireland and on the Irish Volunteers. The seemingly imminent threat of a civil war quickly dissipated as the majority of the UVF joined up to fight in the British Army. However, those on the republican side were faced with a dilemma: fight with Britain against Germany and her allies with the promise that Home Rule would be established in Ireland following the war, or use the opportunity created by the war to force a radical change within Ireland.

On 18 September 1914 John Redmond and the IPP seemed to have finally realised their ambition to win legislative independence for Ireland when the Third Home Rule Act received Royal Assent, an event celebrated with bonfires across southern Ireland. As such, Redmond had no qualms about urging the Irish Volunteers to support Britain's war against Germany. However, more radical elements within the Volunteers were strongly opposed to Redmond's willingness to bolster the old enemy.

Tensions within the organisation boiled over following Redmond's contentious speech at Woodenbridge in Co. Wicklow on 20 September, in which he urged all available Irishmen, including the Irish Volunteers, to enlist in an Irish Army Corps within Lord Kitchener's New Army. Redmond's stance ultimately caused a massive split in the Irish Volunteers, which by then numbered nearly 190,000 men. The vast majority accepted Redmond's call to arms and formed the National Volunteers, with approximately 24,000 joining the British Army in 1914. However, the devastation of the war, coupled with the postponement of Home Rule, greatly diminished Redmond's popularity, and, by the time of the Easter Rising, the National Volunteers as an organisation was all but dead.

Meanwhile, between 9,700 and 11,000 Irish Volunteers refused to follow Redmond and continued on as a closely knit cadre, with Eoin MacNeill as Chief of Staff, The O'Rahilly as his Director of Arms, J. J. O'Connell as Chief of Inspection and Bulmer Hobson as quartermaster. The IRB had also re-established a strong foothold in the organisation through its rising stars Thomas MacDonagh (Director of Training), Éamonn Ceannt (Director of Communications), Patrick Pearse (Director of Military Organisation) and Joe Plunkett (Director of Military Operations).[2] The IRB was more determined than ever that the Irish Volunteers should embark upon an armed offensive against the British authorities in Ireland.

Overleaf: John Redmond addressing a British Army recruiting meeting.

Tom Kettle

Tom Kettle was born in Artane, north Dublin, in 1880, shortly after his father, Andy Kettle, co-founded the Irish Land League in Castlebar, Co. Mayo. After Parnell's death, the elder Kettle bowed out of politics and focused instead on his farm in Finglas, north Dublin, where Tom spent his childhood. An attentive, quick-witted and mischievous schoolboy, the younger Kettle impressed his peers at UCD, where he won a gold medal for oratory and became auditor of the Literary and Historical Society.

As a student he was an outspoken critic of the British during their war with the Boers. He later abandoned a promising legal career to co-found the Young Ireland Branch of the United Irish League. In 1906 John Redmond persuaded him to stand for parliament as an IPP candidate and, at the age of twenty-six, Kettle was elected MP for East Tyrone. Many considered him a shoo-in to succeed Redmond as and when the older man stepped down. Kettle's mindset was always closely entwined with Europe. 'My only programme for Ireland,' he declared, 'consists in equal parts of Home Rule and the Ten Commandments. My only counsel to Ireland is, that to become deeply Irish, she must become European.'[3]

Having been appointed first Professor of National Economics at UCD in 1908, Kettle left the political arena. However, the Dub-liner continued to be an active supporter of Home Rule and was a co-founder of the Irish Volunteers. He was in Belgium to collect a consignment of guns for the organisation when the First World War broke out. He condemned Germany as 'guilty of a systematic campaign of murder, pillage, outrage, and destruction, planned and ordered by her military and intellectual leaders'.[4]

Commissioned as an officer in the Royal Dublin Fusiliers, he threw himself behind the campaign to get Irishmen to enlist in the army, opining that if 'Prussian barbarity' won the war, all talk of Home Rule would be canned. 'It is a confession to make and I make it,' he said. 'I care for liberty more than I care for Ireland.'[5] Like many moderate nationalists, he believed that a united effort by the National Volunteers and the UVF to defeat Germany would bond the two sides and stem the dreaded civil war that seemed so inevitable in 1914.

The Easter Rising was a blow for him on many levels, not least because he was close to many of the rebel leaders. He had served with

Joe Plunkett on the Peace Committee during the 1913 Lockout and with both Thomas MacDonagh and Patrick Pearse on the board of the Theatre of Ireland. His brother Lawrence also took part in the Rising. Tom Kettle was livid with the rebels for destroying what he saw as the best chance for reconciliation between Protestant Ulster and the rest of Ireland. However, as his wife later said, 'what really seared his heart was the fearful retribution that fell on the leaders of the rebellion'.[6] He was also profoundly shaken by the murder of his brother-in-law and college friend Francis Sheehy-Skeffington, killed on the orders of a crazed British officer during the course of the Rising.[7] It didn't help when Kettle went to console his bereaved sister-in-law and her children clad in the same uniform Francis's killer had worn. 'The Sinn Féin nightmare upset me a little,' he wrote later, 'but then if you tickle the ear of an elephant with a pop-gun, and he walks on you, that is a natural concatenation of events.'[8]

In July 1916 Kettle sailed for France where he joined his battalion. He was killed during a charge at German lines during the battle of Ginchy on 9 September. Three days before his death, he penned a sonnet entitled 'To My Daughter Betty, the Gift of God', written in a field near Guillemont. The poem concludes with the lines:

> Know that we fools, now with the foolish dead,
> Died not for flag, nor King, nor Emperor,
> But for a dream, born in a herdsman's shed,
> And for the secret Scripture of the poor.

O'DONOVAN ROSSA'S FUNERAL

Arguably the most important event for Irish republicanism before the 1916 Rising took place in August 1915, with the funeral in Glasnevin Cemetery, Dublin, of the 'unrepentant Fenian' Jeremiah O'Donovan Rossa, a veteran of the 1867 Rising, who had died in a hospital on Staten Island, New York. Planned by Tom Clarke, choreographed by Thomas MacDonagh and defined by Patrick Pearse's epic graveside oration, the funeral brilliantly encapsulated the zeitgeist of a country on the cusp of revolution. It was a spectacle that lived forever in the memory of any who participated on that summer's day.

All the main bodies from the nationalist and socialist cause were represented at the funeral, which took place after Clarke and John Devoy successfully shipped O'Donovan Rossa's body back to Dublin. Among those who marched behind his hearse were the soldiers and pipe bands of the Irish Volunteers, the ICA and Fianna Éireann, as well as manifold members of Redmond's National Volunteers, the Hibernian Rifles, Sinn Féin, the GAA and Cumann na mBan. Dubliners were duly treated to a magnificent procession as these assorted groups marched on a circuitous route through the main streets of the capital from City Hall, where O'Donovan Rossa lay in state for three days, to Glasnevin Cemetery.

Addressing the mourners at O'Donovan Rossa's funeral, Pearse told them that he spoke 'on behalf of a new generation that has been re-baptised in the Fenian faith and that has accepted the responsibility of carrying out the Fenian programme'. His final words were a powerful indication of the growing republican fervour in Ireland, and concluded with an implicit threat against the island's ruling elite:

> The Defenders of this Realm have worked well in secret and in the open. They think that they have pacified Ireland. They think that they have purchased half of us and intimidated the other half. They think that they have foreseen everything, think that they have provided against everything; but, the fools, the fools, the fools! They have left us our Fenian dead, and while Ireland holds these graves, Ireland unfree shall never be at peace.[9]

Opposite: A rather prophetic pen sketch from New York entitled 'The Dawn of Irish Freedom'. It is dated 4–5 March 1916, a full fifty days before the Rising.

Overleaf: Mourners gather by Jeremiah O'Donovan Rossa's graveside in Glasnevin Cemetery. Patrick Pearse, uniformed, stands on the right of the frame, head bowed and holding his hat, with Major John MacBride behind him. Among others identified here are Tom MacDonagh, Seán McGarry, Darrell Figgis, Seán T. O'Kelly, Michael O'Hanrahan, Tom Clarke, Cathal Brugha, Arthur Griffith, Count Plunkett and Fathers Albert Bibby and Aloysius Travers.

Patrick Poarse

Patrick Pearse, or Pádraig MacPhiarais as he sometimes called himself, was one of the seminal figures of the Easter Rising. He was born at 27 Great Brunswick Street (now Pearse Street) in 1879. His father, James Pearse, a stonemason from Birmingham, England, moved to Dublin during the 1860s and set up his monumental sculpture works on Great Brunswick Street, two doors up from the British Army recruiting office. His firm specialised in altarpieces, monuments and ornamental features of considerable beauty. Subsequently known as 'Pearse & Sons', it became the largest monumental sculpture firm in Ireland, employing up to eighty-six workers by the time of James's death.

Patrick and his brother, Willie, were James's sons by his second wife, Dublin-born Margaret Brady.[10] They were educated locally in Wentworth Place (now Hogan Place) and at the Christian Brothers' School on Westland Row. Inspired by his Irish-speaking mother, Patrick became an early adherent to Home Rule and the Gaelic League. In 1903 the twenty-three-year-old became editor of the League's newspaper, *An Claidheamh Soluis*.

Ill at ease in the presence of women, Pearse preferred the company of men and boys.[11] In 1908 he set up Scoil Éanna in Ranelagh, south Dublin, a pioneering school that educated boys through the Irish language. The school was relocated to the Hermitage in Rathfarnham, south Dublin, two years later.

In 1913 the fervently Catholic Pearse co-founded the Irish Volunteers and, after the split with Redmond, he became their Director of Military Organisation. In December 1913 he was sworn into the IRB by Bulmer Hobson. He was then co-opted onto the Supreme Council by Tom Clarke and sent on a fund-raising mission to the USA.

Following his stirring graveside oration at O'Donovan Rossa's funeral in August 1915, Pearse became one of the key architects of the impending insurrection. Along with Willie, he followed James Connolly and Joe Plunkett into the GPO on Easter Monday. As president of the Provisional Government of the Irish Republic, the thirty-six-year-old was theoretically commander-in-chief of the republican forces, although he appears to have bowed in this regard to James Connolly. Six days later, horrified by the mounting civilian casualties, Pearse issued the order to surrender.

He was stoic to the end, penning a moving poem called 'The Mother' in his cell the night before he died and whistling en route from the cell to his place of execution. Willie was executed exactly twenty-four hours later.

'The Mother'

I do not grudge them: Lord, I do not grudge
My two strong sons that I have seen go out
To break their strength and die, they and a few,
In bloody protest for a glorious thing,
They shall be spoken of among their people,
The generations shall remember them,
And call them blessed;
But I will speak their names to my own heart
In the long nights;
The little names that were familiar once
Round my dead hearth.
Lord, thou art hard on mothers:
We suffer in their coming and their going;
And tho' I grudge them not, I weary, weary
Of the long sorrow – And yet I have my joy:
My sons were faithful, and they fought.

ALLIANCE WITH GERMANY AND THE CAPTURE OF SIR ROGER CASEMENT

The first major act of the Easter Rising took place not in Dublin but on the northern shores of Co. Kerry, when a German submarine attempted to deliver its cargo of 20,000 rifles to the Irish Volunteers. The shipment was organised by Sir Roger Casement, a prominent British diplomat, and was regarded by the organisers of the Easter Rising as critical to the success or failure of their rebellion. However, a combination of poor planning and terrible luck meant that the mission ended in spectacular catastrophe on Good Friday, with three Irish Volunteers dead, the German guns sunk in Cork harbour and Casement bound for the gallows.

Before the First World War, Sir Roger Casement was considered Britain's foremost human-rights activist. Born in Dublin to a Protestant father and a Catholic mother, he journeyed to the Congo Free State in Africa as a young man. He stayed there for twenty years, rising to the position of British consul. For a short period he shared a room with Joseph Conrad, whose experiences of the Congo inspired him to write the novel *Heart of Darkness* upon which the film *Apocalypse Now* is based.

Casement's 1904 report on the Congo exposed appalling atrocities on the rubber plantations, in which hundreds of thousands of people died in order to provide rubber for the Belgian-owned companies that were supplying the rapidly expanding automobile industry with tyres. He laid the blame squarely at the feet of Leopold II, King of the Belgians, a first cousin of Queen Victoria and reputedly the richest man in the world. Leopold ruled the Congo as a personal fiefdom with his own private mercenary army. Such was the outrage following Casement's report that Leopold was forced to relinquish control over his mini-kingdom.

Casement subsequently visited the remote Putumayo region on the Colombia–Peru border and cracked open another ghastly case of exploitation, torture and murder, this time run by the Peruvian Amazon Company (PAC), a rubber firm consolidated in London and backed by British shareholders. The Putumayo, where PAC was headquartered, was a no-man's land full of wild rubber trees as well as more than 50,000 Bora, Andoke, Huitoto and Ocaina Indians. Casement estimated that during the first decade of the twentieth century 30,000 of these indigenous inhabitants

Roger Casement, studio portrait, *c.* 1910–16.

had been murdered or deliberately starved to death. For this heavy toll, PAC received 4,000 tons of rubber.

In June 1911 Casement received a knighthood from George V in recognition of his humanitarian work. As part of his campaign to highlight the atrocities, he bought Ricudo and Omarino, two young rubber workers, to London, parading them before Britain's elite as prime exhibits of imperialism gone rotten. He wrote to Patrick Pearse about the possibility of enrolling Omarino at Scoil Éanna, Pearse's progressive, Irish-speaking school in south Dublin. Pearse earnestly replied that he would certainly do his best to 'make a success of the young barbarian'.[12] However, when asked about London, the Amazonians remarked that it was 'very beautiful … but the great river and the forest where the birds fly is more beautiful … one day we shall go back'.[13] Casement returned to the Putumayo with both Amazonians later that same year.

His experiences in the Congo and the Amazon convinced him that colonialism was intrinsically evil. In 1913 he co-founded the Irish Volunteers and began raising money for the cause in the USA. In October 1914 he made his way secretly to Germany where he attempted to form an Irish Brigade from Irish prisoners willing to wear a German uniform and fight the British. However, just fifty-six men volunteered, and the Germans never took Casement's brigade seriously.

Casement's hopes to persuade the Germans to send an armed force to Ireland were also dashed, but he did manage to arrange for a large consignment of rifles, machine guns, explosives and ammunition to be sent to Ireland on the *Aud* ahead of the Rising. He travelled separately on board the German U-19, with Robert Monteith and Julian Bailey (who used the alias Sergeant Daniel Beverley in the Irish Brigade), departing from the German naval base at Heligoland, a small archipelago in the North Sea, and arriving on the north coast of Kerry five days later.

The three men opted to row ashore when it became apparent that neither the *Aud* nor the pilot boat were in Tralee Bay as planned. In the hours

Photo taken on the German submarine U-19 during Casement's journey to Ireland *c.* 20 April 1916. Standing on the deck are Captain Raimund Weisbach (*front right*), while the back row (*left to right*) comprises Robert Monteith, Julian Bailey, Lieutenant Otto Walter and Roger Casement. Casement had just shaved off his distinctive beard, leaving only his moustache, and, like Monteith, he wears a typically Irish peak cap.

before dawn on Good Friday, they clambered out of U-19's conning tower and boarded a collapsible rowing boat with some basic food, maps and sidearms. It took just over an hour – and a near fatal capsizing – for them to combat the dark, rolling ocean and land upon the open sandy beach of Banna Strand from which St Brendan the Navigator is said to have sailed in another age.

Two officers from the RIC stand beside the collapsible rowboat which Casement, Monteith and Bailey used to reach the Kerry coast.

At length, they drew up in the old rath at Currahane (now called Casement's Fort) near Ardfert, where the exhausted Casement lay down to rest while the other two sought help. Monteith managed to evade capture and inform Austin Stack of Casement's arrival, while Bailey made it to Tralee, where he was arrested the following day. However, locals who had watched them come ashore alerted the local RIC, and early in the afternoon, before the Kerry Volunteers could get to him, Casement was arrested, ultimately being charged with treason, sabotage and espionage against the crown.

Roger Casement at his trial in Bow Street Court, London, c. May–June 1916. Press coverage of Casement's trial, and his subsequent execution, inspired the modernist poet Thomas MacGreevy to write his first work of fiction – a dialogue between the imprisoned Casement and a senior British politician.

Casement's trial was one of the most controversial of its time. The solicitor George Gavan Duffy was dismissed by his law firm for agreeing to defend him. During the trial, the British authorities leaked a number of stories describing homosexual encounters that were alleged to have come from private journals written by Casement. The so-called Black Diaries were part of a campaign to turn public sentiment against him. The fifty-one-year-old was hanged by John Ellis and his assistants at Pentonville Prison in London on 3 August 1916.

Witnesses gathered outside the court at Bow Street for Casement's trial.

words were "Into thy hands O Lord. I commend my spirit. Lord Jesu receive my soul."
Lady Constance Emmott says she remembers him as a clever & delightful friend. She would have found him unchanged had she been able to visit him in his condemned cell. Those who ever called him friend kept their good opinion of him to the end. There are still many things to say, and many others to write so I must conclude, asking you & Lady Constance Emmott to remember his soul in your kind prayers Yours Sincerely James McCarroll

Extract from a letter written by Fr James McCarroll, the confessor who was in the cell with Roger Casement before his execution. He opined that Casement was 'a saint … we should be praying to him instead of for him'.

John Devoy

The veteran Clan na Gael leader John Devoy (*right*) pictured with Sir Roger Casement in the USA in 1914.

Born near Kill, Co. Kildare, John Devoy lived a colourful life, spending a year with the French Foreign Legion in Algeria before becoming one of the senior figures of the Fenian Brotherhood. He later moved to the USA and became a journalist for the *New York Herald*. Following the outbreak of the First World War, the elderly Devoy – then head of Clan na Gael – met with Sir Roger Casement and Count von Bernstorff, the German ambassador to the USA and Mexico, to discuss the possibility of a rebellion in Ireland supported by German arms, money and military counsel. The meeting ultimately led to Roger Casement's doomed arms mission in April 1916.

Captain Robert Monteith

Captain Robert Monteith (1879–1956) *c.* 1914–15 in the uniform of the Irish Volunteers.

Robert 'Bob' Monteith was the third son of a Protestant farmer from Newtownmountkennedy, Co. Wicklow. In 1894 he joined the British Army, serving variously in the Khyber Pass, Egypt and South Africa. During the Anglo-Boer War, Bombardier Monteith was apparently the second man to ride through the blockade for the relief of Ladysmith. He later left the army and settled in Dublin, where he married and found work at the Ordnance Depot at Islandbridge.

Family lore holds that he became radicalised during the 1913 Lockout, when his sister-in-law ventured out on a shopping trip only to be beaten up by a baton-wielding constable. Monteith joined the Irish Volunteers at the first opportunity. When he refused to rejoin the British Army on the outbreak of the First World War, he was dismissed from his post at the Ordnance Depot. He moved to Limerick, where he began organising and drilling the local Volunteers.

On Tom Clarke's orders, he went to Germany in October 1915 to command Casement's Irish Brigade. Five months later, he and Julian Bailey, a Dublin-born Irish Brigade sergeant, joined Casement for the ill-fated gun-run to Ireland.

While Casement and Bailey were captured, Monteith managed to evade the authorities and escaped to New York in December 1916. He later became a fund-raiser for de Valera and played a prominent role in the American Association for the Recognition of the Irish Republic. Based in Detroit, he served as foreman in the Ford Motor Company plant at Dearborn, Michigan, for twenty years.

In 1947 he and his wife, Mollie, returned to Ireland, despite words of caution from de Valera who wrote, 'It is hard to transplant the oak at seventy … I can't see why you are coming over here, there is nothing for you.' Monteith replied, 'I am coming home under my own steam. I ask nothing of any man.'[14] The Monteiths spent six years in Ireland, living variously between Kilcoole, Co. Wicklow, Sutton, Co. Dublin and Donnycarney, on the north side of Dublin city, before Mollie persuaded her husband to return to the USA in 1953. Bob Monteith died in Detroit three years later, at the age of seventy-seven.

Captain Raimund Weisbach

Captain Raimund Weisbach (1886–1970) was commander of U-19, the submarine that carried Casement to Ireland. Born in Breslau, Silesia, Weisbach formerly served as the watch officer on board the German U-boat U-20, which infamously torpedoed the ocean-liner RMS *Lusitania* off the Old Head of Kinsale on 7 May 1915, resulting in the deaths of 1,201 passengers and crew. Weisbach, who was awarded the Iron Cross 1st Class, watched the torpedo strike through a periscope, and the magnitude of the blast convinced him that the supposedly neutral *Lusitania* was illicitly carrying high explosives to assist the British war effort. As a U-boat commander, Weisbach sank thirty-six ships before his submarine was sunk by the Royal Navy in May 1917. Imprisoned in Britain, he later returned to Germany, where he died in Hamburg in 1970. In 1966 he was an official guest of the Irish government at the commemoration of the fiftieth anniversary of the Rising.

Count von Bernstorff, the German Ambassador

Johann Heinrich von Bernstorff served as German ambassador to the USA and Mexico from 1908 to 1917 and was closely involved with the initial plot to bring German arms to Ireland. His father had been one of the most powerful politicians in the Prussian Empire until he was outmanoeuvred by Otto von Bismarck and dispatched to London as ambassador at the Court of St James. The younger Bernstorff, who co-founded the German Democratic Party after the First World War, was later named by Adolf Hitler as one of those who bore 'the guilt and responsibility for the collapse of Germany'. When the Nazis came to power in 1933, he wisely fled to Geneva, Switzerland, where he died in 1939.

THE SS *AUD*

On 9 April 1916, the steamer *Aud* sailed from the Baltic port of Lübeck, bound for the south-west coast of Ireland. Built in Hull, Yorkshire, and initially called SS *Castro*, the steamer had been seized by the Imperial German Navy in the Kiel Canal at the start of the First World War and

The ship *Castro*, renamed the *Aud* and sent to Ireland with the German arms shipment for the 1916 Rising.

renamed *Libau*. On the Casement expedition, she adopted the guise of a Norwegian timber carrier called SS *Aud-Norge*.

As well as twenty-two crew, the *Aud* carried 20,000 rifles, including modern Lee Enfields and Mausers, along with ten light machine guns, 1 million rounds of ammunition and 400 kilogrammes of explosives. Reserve-Lieutenant Karl Spindler, a quarry owner's son from Cologne, was the man entrusted with bringing Casement's armaments to Ireland. Over the course of eleven days, he skippered the SS *Aud-Norge* from the Baltic to Tralee Bay.

The ship evaded patrols by the British 10th Cruiser Squadron and weathered two violent storms off Rockall to reach Tralee Bay on Thursday 20 April. However, the plan to transfer the cargo to the Irish Volunteers fell apart due to a combination of bad luck, poor planning and communication breakdown. Austin Stack, a former secretary of the Kerry GAA County Board and commandant of the Kerry Brigade of the Irish Volunteers, was entrusted with the task of meeting the *Aud*, unloading the weapons and distributing the arms. However, he was not expecting the ship until Easter Saturday, so when Captain Spindler sailed into Tralee Bay two days earlier, there was no one there to receive his cargo and he had no way of contacting the local Volunteers.

In fact, the Volunteers had an ambitious plan to establish communication with the arms ship. Assuming the *Aud* would arrive on Saturday, a five-man unit left Dublin on Good Friday and made their way south to Killarney, Co. Kerry, where they were picked up by Limerick Volunteers Thomas McInerney and Sammy Windrim. The plan was for the men to drive to Valentia Island and seize control of the wireless station. Having taken the station, the men were to alert the Royal Navy that the German Imperial Navy was about to invade Scotland, thus generating much confusion among the ships patrolling the coast of south-west Ireland. They would simultaneously establish contact with the *Aud* and guide her and her cargo in to meet Austin Stack's Volunteers waiting on the Kerry shore.[15]

Captain Karl Spindler (1887–1951), commander of the *Aud* and author of *The Mystery of the Casement Ship*. Portrait photograph taken in Germany *c.* 1916.

Hans Dunker (1891–1978), a stoker with the Kriegsmarine, was another member of the *Aud*'s crew.

McInerney was the chauffeur for Con Keating, Charlie Monaghan and Dan Sheehan that fateful evening. Keating hailed from Cahirsiveen and had served as a radio officer on various ships, while Monaghan was a wireless installation expert. Sheehan had worked at the War Office and knew the vital Admiralty codes. Tragically, on the journey from Killarney to Valentia, McInerney took a wrong turn in the dark and drove off the pier at Ballykissane, near Killorglin. The driver escaped, but his three passengers drowned in the River Laune, becoming the first casualties in the 1916 Rising. McInerney was arrested shortly afterwards and following the Rising was transferred to the Frongoch internment camp near Bala in north Wales. Upon his release, he rejoined the IRA. He was accidentally killed in Co. Tipperary in 1922.

Even if these Volunteers had succeeded in taking the Valentia station, they would have been too late to save the situation, as earlier on that same Good Friday, the *Aud* had been trapped in Tralee bay by a blockade of British ships. British Naval Intelligence had intercepted messages between Clan na Gael and the German ambassador in the USA concerning the ship's journey and had been on the lookout for her. While the *Aud* was being escorted towards the naval base at Cobh (then Queenstown), Karl Spindler instructed his crew to scuttle the ship at the entrance to Cork harbour, where her remains lie to this day.

Having scuttled the ship, Spindler and his crew were briefly interned on Spike Island in Cork harbour, before being transported to a prisoner-of-war camp in England for the remainder of the First World War. Spindler subsequently moved to the USA, where he embarked on a lecture tour, speaking of his epic trip to Ireland and his connections with the Easter Rising. He died in Bismarck, North Dakota, in 1951.

Austin Stack is pictured here with nine fellow members of the Kerry Brigade at the Sportsfield (now Austin Stack Park) in Tralee, Co. Kerry.

Front row (left to right): Danny Healy, Austin Stack (commandant), Alfred Cotton.

Middle row: Michael Doyle, Frank Roche, Danny Mullins, Eddie Barry.

Back row: Joe Mellin, Ned Lynch, Mick Flemming.

The car in which Con Keating, Charlie Mona-ghan and Dan Sheehan were travelling towards Valentia Island to make contact with the *Aud* when it drove off Ballykissane Pier on Good Friday 1916, killing all three of them.

Diarmuid Lynch

Born near Tracton, Co. Cork, Diarmuid Lynch was working as a clerk at the Mount Pleasant Money Order Office in London when he accepted the offer of a job from an uncle in New York. By 1897 the nineteen-year-old was secretary of the New York Philo-Celtic Society, which sought to promote the Irish language in North America. Membership quadrupled on his watch. He became an American citizen as well as state president of the Gaelic League of the State of New York.

In 1907 Lynch returned to Ireland to work for a large wholesaler of agricultural supplies in Dublin. Invited to join the IRB by Seán T. O'Kelly, he was elected Munster representative on the Supreme Council in 1911. Only two men, Lynch and Michael Collins, held positions of power in the three main nationalist organisations – the IRB, the Irish Volunteers and Sinn Féin – at the same time. And of these two, it was Lynch who was intimately involved in the planning for the Rising.

On Patrick Pearse's command Lynch went to Tralee, and it was he who selected Fenit as the best place for Roger Casement to land his cargo of German arms. Lynch was present on Easter Saturday when the Rising's leaders decided to push ahead despite Eoin Mac-Neill's countermand. He served as aide-de-camp to James Connolly in the GPO, and he was reputedly the last man to leave the building when it was evacuated. Lynch would probably have been executed but for his American citizenship.

In 1918 he was elected TD in the First Dáil for Cork South-East, despite the fact he had been deported to the USA earlier that year. In America, he worked passionately as National Secretary of the Friends of Irish Freedom, an organisation that had already raised $350,000 to assist dependants of those who had fought in the Rising. He retained the office until his resignation in 1920 amid sharp differences with de Valera as to how such funds should be spent. His important role in the Easter Rising was subsequently obscured from history.[16]

Blinker Hall's Naval Intelligence

Rear Admiral Sir William 'Blinker' Hall was Britain's Director of Naval Intelligence. Among the missives his team intercepted were those between John Devoy of Clan na Gael and the German general staff that led directly to the capture of the *Aud*. The same communiqués also led to the arrest of Roger Casement. Hall, who personally interrogated Casement, is said to have rejected the former consul's pleas for a chance to publicly urge the leaders of the projected Rising to call it off.

MacNEILL'S COUNTERMAND, EASTER SUNDAY 1916

Eoin MacNeill, Chief of Staff of the Irish Volunteers, was kept in the dark about the planned Rising by its leaders. When he first learned of the plans on Good Friday, he initially allowed himself to be talked into it by Seán Mac Diarmada, who explained that Germany was on side, that a large consignment of arms was due to arrive at any moment and that the rebellion would commence on Easter Sunday when Irish Volunteers across Ireland gathered for parades and manoeuvres.

On Easter Saturday MacNeill was informed that Roger Casement and the German arms had been captured in Kerry. He hastily penned an eleven-word countermanding order on headed notepaper, at his home in Rathfarnham, Co. Dublin, and dispatched copies to local commanders nationwide. The message read: 'Volunteers completely deceived. All orders for tomorrow, Sunday, are completely cancelled.' He then made his way to the offices of the *Sunday Independent*, which published his order the following morning.

MacNeill's countermand overruled previous orders issued by the IRB Military Council, thus effectively calling the rebellion off. The Council members were deeply dismayed by MacNeill's actions but felt they had already waded too far across the river to turn back. They quickly began to circulate word through their own channels that the Rising would now take place on Easter Monday instead. All of this caused considerable confusion among Volunteers across Ireland, not least in Cork and Limerick, where there was consequently no rebellion.

Christopher Brady, a printer on the staff of the *Workers' Republic*, recalled seeing a furious Constance Markievicz arriving into Liberty Hall with MacNeill's countermand and announcing, 'I will shoot Eoin MacNeill.' James Connolly replied, 'You are not to hurt a hair on MacNeill's head. If anything happens to MacNeill I will hold you responsible.'[17]

Mac Diarmada's assurance of German support was not without foundation. On the evening of Easter Monday, a squadron of German battlecruisers fired on the British coastal ports of Yarmouth and Lowestoft while zeppelins dropped bombs along England's east coast. This was deliberately timed to serve as both a support action and a diversion for the Easter Rising.[18]

Overleaf: Based on a large photogravure print after W. G. Rogers, this painting from 1917 shows the sixteen men who were executed in the wake of the Easter Rising seated and standing around a table, with a harp and crossed flags in the background. Sir Roger Casement and Tom Kent are represented as pictures hanging on the wall in Hogarthian frames.

Seated (left to right): Patrick Pearse, John MacBride, Tom Clarke, Éamonn Ceannt, James Connolly and Joe Plunkett.

Standing: Willie Pearse, Thomas MacDonagh, Seán Heuston, Michael Mallin, Seán Mac Diarmada, Michael O'Hanrahan, Edward Daly, Con Colbert.

Seán Mac Diarmada

Seán Mac Diarmada clearly enjoyed filling out the census form in April 1911. At the time he was lodging at 15 Russell Place on Dublin's North Circular Road. He filled out the form in Irish, naming himself 'Seaghán Mac Diarmada'. Under 'Marriage' the twenty-six-year-old remarked 'Single, but not for long', and under 'Disabilities' he wrote 'heart-broken from being single'. Under 'Religion' he entered 'Náisiuntacht na h-Éireann', meaning 'The Nationhood of Ireland'. This was helpfully but erroneously translated by the enumerator as 'Church of Ireland'.

Two Examples of the mode of filling up this Table are given on the other side.

FORM A.

No. on Form B. 15

RETURN of the MEMBERS of this FAMILY and their VISITORS, BOARDERS, SERVANTS, &c., who slept or abode in this House on the night of SUNDAY, the 2nd of APRIL, 1911.

NAME AND SURNAME		RELATION to Head of Family.	RELIGIOUS PROFESSION.	EDUCATION.	AGE (last Birthday) and SEX.		RANK, PROFESSION, OR OCCUPATION.	PARTICULARS AS TO MARRIAGE.				WHERE BORN.	IRISH LANGUAGE.	If Deaf and Dumb; Dumb only; Blind; Imbecile or Idiot; or Lunatic.
Christian Name.	Surname.				Ages of Males	Ages of Females		Whether "Married," "Widower," "Widow," or "Single."	Completed years the present Marriage has lasted.	Children born alive. Total Children born alive.	Children still living.			
1 Elizabeth	Dunn	Head of Family	Catholic	Read & Write	32		House holder	Widow	—	—	—	Co. Mayo	English	
2 Mary	Langan	Sister	Catholic	Read & Write		31	Dress Maker	Married	4	1	1	Co. Mayo	English	
4 Patricia	Langan	Niece	Catholic	Read & Write		9	Scholar					Dublin City	English	
6 Coirneagán	Ó Coileáin	Visitor	Catholic	Can read & Write	28	—	Cléireac	Single	—	—	—	Co. Luimnig	Gaeilge / English	
8 Seaghán	Mac Diarmada	Visitor	Catholic				Cléireac Clk	Single	—	—	—	Co. Liatroma	Gaeilge / English	
10 Pádraig	Ó Murgaileasig	Visitor	Catholic	Can read & Write	19		Cléireac Clk	Single	—	—	—	Cúige mara	Gaeilge / English	
12 Úna	Ní Éilir					17		Single	—	—	—	Co. Mayo	Gaeilge / English	
13 Muiréad	Ní Éilir					19		Single	—	—	—	Co. Mayo	Gaeilge / English	

Seán Mac Diarmada's 1911 census form.

Mac Diarmada, the eighth of ten children, was born in 1883 in a small thatched cottage on the Tottenham estate near Kiltyclogher in the impoverished north of Co. Leitrim. His Irish-speaking father, Donald, a carpenter and part-time farmer, was an old friend of the veteran Fenian John Daly. His mother, Mary, died when he was nine. As a teenager, he abandoned his ambitions to become a schoolteacher and instead found work raking and digging gardens with a cousin in Edinburgh, where he became a fan of Robbie Burns' poetry. He also entertained his pals with his rendition of Robert Emmet's 'Speech from the Dock', which he had memorised word for word. Another early indication of his political sympathies concerns his greyhound Kruger, named for Paul Kruger, the Boer general who took on the British in the Anglo-Boer War.

In 1905 Mac Diarmada moved to the rapidly industrialising city of Belfast, home to the largest shipbuilding yards in the world.

He found lodging in the Ardoyne area and a job as a conductor on the tramway system, poorly paid but steady. Within a year he had become friendly with Bulmer Hobson and Denis McCullough, with whom he organised the nationalist Dungannon Clubs. Mac Diarmada was also sworn into the IRB and became exceptionally active in the Gaelic League. In 1907 he was appointed Sinn Féin's organiser and Director of Elections in the north Leitrim area.

Mac Diarmada moved to Dublin in 1908 to help Tom Clarke, lately returned from New York, to restructure and ultimately take over the IRB. He travelled extensively across Ireland for much of the next three years, recruiting new members to the cause. The handsome, dark-haired, blue-eyed Leitrim man became a very well-known face – particularly to the police, who were constantly on his tail. Although he describes himself as a mere 'clerk' on the 1911 census, he was by then managing the radical newspaper *Irish Freedom*, which he co-founded with Hobson and McCullough.

In September 1911, five months after he filled out the census form, Mac Diarmada was struck with polio, or 'infantile paralysis', which caused him severe lameness in his right leg, and he was obliged to walk with a cane thereafter. In addition to painful neuralgia, he also developed bladder issues. He spent some four months in the Mater Hospital and then recuperated at the homes of various fellow republicans over the following year.

From 1912 until the Rising, Mac Diarmada and Clarke formed a two-man executive on the IRB's Supreme Council. On account of his ailments, Seán was unable to play an active military role in the Rising itself. Nonetheless, he was stationed at the GPO and signed the Proclamation of Independence. Along with Willie Pearse, he was the only senior figure who did not cry when Patrick Pearse surrendered.

Mac Diarmada faced two charges, to which he pleaded not guilty, namely that he:

1. … did take part in an armed rebellion and in the waging of war against His Majesty the King, such act being of such a nature as to be calculated to be prejudicial to the Defence of the Realm and being done with the intention and for the purpose of assisting the enemy.

2. … did attempt to cause disaffection among the civilian population of His Majesty.[19]

He was executed by firing squad on 12 May 1916 at the age of thirty-three. Before his execution, he wrote, 'I feel happiness the like of which I have never experienced. I die that the Irish nation might live!' Those words now adorn a statue of him in his home village of Kiltyclogher. Busáras – Dublin's main bus station – is officially named Áras Mhic Dhiarmada in his honour.

Mac Diarmada never did find a wife, although he was very close to Min Ryan at the time of the Rising. She later married General Richard Mulcahy, who played a prominent part in the War of Independence that followed 1916. Min's sister Agnes was married to Dinny McCullough, president of the IRB, while her other sisters, Mary Kate and Phyllis, were both married, in turn, to fellow revolutionary and future Irish president, Seán T. O'Kelly. Min's brother, James Ryan, was medical officer in the GPO during the Rising and later served as a long-standing Fianna Fáil minister.

DUBLIN
RISES

THE BATTLE COMMENCES

The first fatal shots of the Easter Rising were fired when approximately 'twenty reliable young men' from Fianna Éireann, assisted by a small number of Irish Volunteers, attacked the Royal Magazine Fort in Phoenix Park at midday on the fine Easter Monday bank holiday, 24 April 1916.[1] The idea for the attack originated with Paddy Daly (also known as O'Daly), a twenty-eight-year-old Volunteer who was working as a contract carpenter at the fort.

Built in 1735, the Magazine Fort was located on St Thomas's Hill, an earthy mound that once belonged to the Knights Hospitaller monks of Kilmainham. It was always something of an oddity, as noted by Jonathan Swift, author of *Gulliver's Travels*, who wrote:

> Now's here's a proof of Irish sense
>
> Here Irish wit is seen
>
> When nothing's left that's worth defence,
>
> We build a Magazine.

Daly was instructed by Seán Mac Diarmada to gather as much information as possible about the fort; much of this was supplied by the fort's storekeeper, whom Daly kept liberally supplied with whiskey. On 16 April, Palm Sunday, Daly gave a summary of his findings to a group at Clontarf Town Hall, including Mac Diarmada, Tom Clarke and Thomas MacDonagh. He also explained how the fort might be captured, which caused Mac Diarmada and Clarke to ask whether he might be able to blow the fort's ammunition and powder store sky-high.[2]

Daly's plan hinged on kitting out the assailants as a football team and then bluffing their way up to the fort; football teams frequently played near the building. As such, the leadership turned to Éamon Martin, the Director of Organisation and Recruiting for Fianna Éireann and commander of its Dublin battalion. Martin had already shown his prowess when, twenty months earlier, he was among those standing on the dark, rain-swept shingle shore of Kilcoole waiting to collect a cargo of 600 German rifles and 20,000 rounds of boxed ammunition from the *Chotah*.

Martin had known of the mission since 17 April, when he met with Daly and Con Colbert. On the evening of Easter Sunday he received his orders directly from James Connolly that he was to attack the fort at 3 p.m. the following day. However, the confusion over whether or not to mobilise was already so rampant that many of 'the lads ... presuming everything was cancelled, had gone hiking or to camps'.[3]

Nonetheless, on the morning of Easter Monday, about twenty Fianna boys arrived at Rutland Street in Summerhill, the home of Garry Holohan, Quartermaster General and Chief of Staff of Fianna Éireann. The scheduled attack had by then been brought forward to midday.

With their numbers low, Martin sought advice from Connolly and Pearse at Liberty Hall. Pearse signed an order requesting a number of his battalion commanders to allocate some of their men to the Fianna. Garry Holohan took this order to Éamonn Ceannt at the South Dublin Union, while Martin and Paddy Holohan, brother of Garry, rounded up some more men from Blackhall Place and elsewhere, making for a grand total of seven or eight Volunteers, including Daly. There were still concerns that there were not enough men, but Clarke silenced many when he remarked: 'Those boys may be light but they are great boys.'[4]

The plan was now in danger of falling behind schedule. Hastily, Martin gathered the unit as one before they advanced towards Phoenix

Park, purchasing a football at Whelan's on Ormond Quay en route. At this juncture, command of the operation passed to Paddy Daly, who had drawn up a plan of attack. Shortly before midday, Daly's men arrived at Phoenix Park and made their way towards the fort, innocuously passing the ball from one to another while shifting ever closer to the sentry on duty. Then, in a flash, they pounced. While Paddy Boland tackled and disarmed the sentry, Daly, Martin and the other men rushed into the fort with pistols and revolvers drawn. The soldiers in the guardroom soon found themselves face to the wall with their arms in the air as the Volunteers gathered up whatever guns and ammunition they found inside. One sentry attempted to resist, but was shot in the leg by Garry Holohan; he subsequently died from his injuries. The soldiers were locked up in the guardroom, along with Georgina Playfair, the wife of the superintendent of the Magazine Fort, and three of her children. Major George Playfair, MC, the superintendent, was fighting on the Western Front at this time, as was their eldest son.

Having located the keys, Daly's men began smashing up ammunition boxes, soaking the rooms with paraffin oil and laying a series of tin-can bombs. When the charge was set, they evacuated the Playfairs from the guardroom and, according to Martin's witness statement, left instructions with the captive soldiers that they could also leave when the last rebels had exited the building. The men then fired the fuses, left the premises and scattered. Martin was among a group who hopped into a waiting hackney car that sped them off towards Islandbridge.

As they came out onto the road at the Islandbridge Gate, they noticed one of the Playfair boys running at full pelt to raise the alarm. Several accounts later stated that George Playfair was a teenager, with some claiming he was just fourteen years old. He was actually twenty-three years old at this time and working as a clerk in the Inland Revenue. As the Volunteers watched, the young man spoke hurriedly with a policeman directing traffic before sprinting down the centre of the road towards No. 1 Park Place, which was the home of the officer commanding the Islandbridge Barracks. There was a telephone in the house.

If George Playfair managed to raise the alarm, then the chances were that the rebels would soon be completely overpowered by soldiers from the Islandbridge and Royal Barracks. The Fianna were also presumably on high alert for activity from Marlborough Barracks (now McKee Barracks), adjoining the park to the south-east, where a considerable force of British yeomanry and cavalry were garrisoned.[5]

Éamon Martin (1892–1971, *left*), with Garry Holohan (1894–1967). Martin was commandant of Fianna Éireann's Dublin Brigade in 1916 and served as Fianna Director of Training and Chief of Staff from 1916 to 1920. Holohan took over as commandant of the Dublin Brigade in 1917 and was also the national Fianna Quartermaster General. Both men had been in the Fianna since the early years and, along with Adjutant-General Barney Mellows, they powered the organisation in the aftermath of the Easter Rising. The photograph was taken between the time of Holohan's return from Frongoch internment camp and Martin's departure for the USA in December 1916.

Garry Holohan, who was cycling alongside the hackney car, weighed up the situation and began to pedal fast. The lady of the house had just opened the door when Holohan cycled up beside them and fired three bullets at point-blank range into George Playfair's abdomen.[6] Playfair, who was born in Halifax, Nova Scotia, was rushed to hospital but died nine hours later.[7]

Shortly after Playfair was shot, the men heard a series of lacklustre explosions from the fort. There are various accounts of why the plan to blow up the building came asunder. A vital key to the gun-cotton store could not be found. Likewise, the high explosives they hoped to find at the fort were not there. Armed with a small gelignite charge, they created a blaze that took a Fire Brigade unit from Thomas Street until midnight to extinguish, largely because the firemen were competing with the random but deadly detonation of several boxes of explosives.[8]

By the time Martin's hackney crossed Kingsbridge Railway Station, the British defences were taking shape; bullets whizzed at the car as it sped up Benburb Street to join Commandant Ned Daly's men at Church Street. Martin carried on to the GPO to update Connolly and Pearse on the situation at the Magazine Fort.[9] He then borrowed The O'Rahilly's De Dion-Bouton motorcar so he could spin back to Garry Holohan's house and pick up the rest of the arms and ammunition. He was thus the last man to drive this iconic car before it was used as a barricade in Prince's Street at the GPO.

Martin was shot the following evening, during an attempt to capture the Broadstone Railway Station, the Dublin terminus of the Midland Great Western Railway. He was taken to Richmond Hospital, from where his old gun-running accomplice, Sir Thomas Myles, would help him escape all the way to the USA.

Paddy Daly was also taken to the Richmond when he was shot in the arm later in the week. Arrested in early June, he was taken to the Bridewell, where the younger Playfair boy identified him as one of those who attacked the Magazine Fort. After the Rising ended Daly was sent to Frongoch.

Tom Clarke

Tom Clarke, the son of a bombardier in the Royal Artillery, was born on the Isle of Wight in 1858 and spent some of his childhood in South Africa. The family moved to Dungannon, Co. Tyrone, in 1865, where his father, James, served with the local militia force. Witnessing the immense poverty of the area, from which Catholics were frequently compelled to emigrate, the younger Clarke became an avid republican. In 1878 he and a friend went to Dublin, where they were sworn into the IRB by John Daly, Head Centre for Connaught.

By 1880 Clarke was living in the USA, where he joined Clan na Gael. In 1883 he volunteered for service in the Fenian dynamite campaign in Britain and was sent to blow up London Bridge. Despite his ship hitting an iceberg en route to Britain and sinking, he made it to Birmingham, but there he was betrayed and arrested while carrying a portmanteau containing an India-rubber stocking 'full of a liquid stated to be a dangerous explosive'.[10] Found guilty of high treason, he spent the next fifteen years in British prisons in Portland and Chatham.

During his incarceration, Clarke strengthened his bond of friendship with John Daly, who was also serving a lifetime sentence for treason and dynamite offences. Suffering from very bad health, Daly was released from Portland in 1897. When Clarke got out in the winter of 1898, he quickly made his way to Limerick to reunite with his comrade. During his time in Limerick, Clarke fell in love with Daly's niece Kathleen, whom he married in New York in 1901. The Clarkes initially lived in Brooklyn before moving to a farm in Long Island, which John Daly financed. Tom, an active member of Clan na Gael in New York, became increasingly keen to return to Ireland, where the republican movement was growing in strength.

In 1907 Tom persuaded Kathleen to return to Dublin, where they opened a tobacconist at 177 Amiens Street and then a stationer's and newsagent on Parnell Street. By 1910 the Clarkes and their three sons were living above the shop on Amiens Street. Times were hard. Kathleen was particularly stressed by the challenges of motherhood and running two shops while her husband plotted revolution with his protégés Bulmer Hobson and Seán Mac Diarmada.

When Hobson helped John Redmond take over the Irish Volunteers in 1914, he was court-martialled by the Supreme Council of the IRB and resigned his seat. Clarke never spoke to him again. Seán McGarry later said that the fallout with Hobson was 'the worst' of 'many, very many grievous disappointments' in Clarke's life.[11] Thereafter, Clarke and Mac Diarmada became virtually inseparable, serving as secretary and treasurer of the IRB. In 1915 the duo completed their conquest of the IRB by establishing the Military Committee that planned the Rising. Clarke, the first man

to sign the Proclamation of the Republic, was stati[...]
throughout Easter Week.

On 3 May the fifty-nine-year-old became the second lead[...] shot by firing squad (Patrick Pearse was the first). Samuel Lomas, [...] member of the firing party, recalled that it required 'a bullet from the officer to complete the ghastly business'.[12]

Shortly before his execution, he asked Kathleen to deliver a 'Message to the Irish People': 'I and my fellow signatories believe we have struck the first successful blow for Irish freedom. The next blow, which we have no doubt Ireland will strike, will win through. In this belief, we die happy.' The statement was printed on a memorial card circulated by Kathleen in the months following her husband's death.

Tomás S. Ó. Cléiriš
(TOM CLARKE),
75a Parnell Street (Next Door to O'Connell Street) and
77 Amiens Street, Dublin.
TOBACCONIST, STATIONER AND NEWSAGENT.
IRISH TOBACCO GOODS A SPECIALITY.

A printed advertisement for Tom Clarke's shops in Dublin, which appeared in a programme for the 'Aonach na Nodlag' (Christmas fair) held at the Rotunda buildings, Dublin, in December 1912. The Aonach was an exhibition for Irish-made products planned by a committee including Arthur Griffith (chairman), Éamonn Ceannt and Tomás Ó Seaghdha (honorary secretaries).

SEIZING THE GPO

Shortly after midday on Easter Monday, a combined force from the Irish Volunteers and the ICA rushed into the General Post Office (GPO), the central telecommunications depot in Ireland. They cleared the public areas, taking a small number of prisoners, including Second Lieutenant Chalmers, an off-duty soldier, who was writing a postcard to his wife at the time. Chalmers was searched for arms, tied up and imprisoned in a telephone booth in the main office.[13] The Volunteers quickly began fortifying the ground floor with anything that came to hand, such as books and ledgers, as well as sandbags, before they gradually seized the entire building, including the telegraph instrument room, the trunk telephone exchange, the sorting offices and other support offices. The GPO staff put up a defence, and a guard in the telegraph room was shot and wounded, but they were quickly overwhelmed.

Meanwhile, Patrick Pearse went out to the front of the GPO and read out the solemn, high-minded Proclamation of Independence by which the Irish Republic was declared as a sovereign, independent state. 'In the name of God and of the dead generations,' declared the Proclamation, 'Ireland, through us, summons her children to her flag and strikes for her freedom … supported by her exiled children in America and by gallant allies in Europe … she strikes in full confidence of victory'.

Seán T. O'Kelly was entrusted with the task of pasting copies of the Proclamation around the city centre. He cannily popped one, addressed to his aunt, into a pillar box beside the GPO. She received her copy shortly after the Rising concluded; it is one of the few copies that survives to the present day.[14]

POBLACHT NA H EIREANN.

THE PROVISIONAL GOVERNMENT
OF THE
IRISH REPUBLIC
TO THE PEOPLE OF IRELAND.

IRISHMEN AND IRISHWOMEN : In the name of God and of the dead generations from which she receives her old tradition of nationhood, Ireland, through us, summons her children to her flag and strikes for her freedom.

Having organised and trained her manhood through her secret revolutionary organisation, the Irish Republican Brotherhood, and through her open military organisations, the Irish Volunteers and the Irish Citizen Army, having patiently perfected her discipline, having resolutely waited for the right moment to reveal itself, she now seizes that moment, and, supported by her exiled children in America and by gallant allies in Europe, but relying in the first on her own strength, she strikes in full confidence of victory.

We declare the right of the people of Ireland to the ownership of Ireland, and to the unfettered control of Irish destinies, to be sovereign and indefeasible. The long usurpation of that right by a foreign people and government has not extinguished the right, nor can it ever be extinguished except by the destruction of the Irish people. In every generation the Irish people have asserted their right to national freedom and sovereignty; six times during the past three hundred years they have asserted it in arms. Standing on that fundamental right and again asserting it in arms in the face of the world, we hereby proclaim the Irish Republic as a Sovereign Independent State, and we pledge our lives and the lives of our comrades-in-arms to the cause of its freedom, of its welfare, and of its exaltation among the nations.

The Irish Republic is entitled to, and hereby claims, the allegiance of every Irishman and Irishwoman. The Republic guarantees religious and civil liberty, equal rights and equal opportunities to all its citizens, and declares its resolve to pursue the happiness and prosperity of the whole nation and of all its parts, cherishing all the children of the nation equally, and oblivious of the differences carefully fostered by an alien government, which have divided a minority from the majority in the past.

Until our arms have brought the opportune moment for the establishment of a permanent National Government, representative of the whole people of Ireland and elected by the suffrages of all her men and women, the Provisional Government, hereby constituted, will administer the civil and military affairs of the Republic in trust for the people.

We place the cause of the Irish Republic under the protection of the Most High God, Whose blessing we invoke upon our arms, and we pray that no one who serves that cause will dishonour it by cowardice, inhumanity, or rapine. In this supreme hour the Irish nation must, by its valour and discipline and by the readiness of its children to sacrifice themselves for the common good, prove itself worthy of the august destiny to which it is called.

Signed on Behalf of the Provisional Government,

THOMAS J. CLARKE.

SEAN Mac DIARMADA.   THOMAS MacDONAGH.
P. H. PEARSE,   EAMONN CEANNT,
JAMES CONNOLLY.   JOSEPH PLUNKETT.

O'Kelly was also probably responsible for pasting another copy of the Proclamation at the foot of Nelson's Pillar. The figure and shaft of this iconic Sackville Street monument were 'thickly studded' with bullets over the week of the Rising, while *The Irish Times* reported that 'one unlucky shot took away the warrior's nose'.[15] The shot was probably fired by John Neale, a London-born sniper with a Cockney accent who served as a lookout with the Hotel Metropole garrison on Sackville Street.[16] From a parapet on the top floor, he apparently kept taking potshots at Nelson's nose until Connolly ordered him to desist. Neale died of wounds received during the evacuation of the Metropole, which was next to the GPO, when a British sniper bullet detonated an ammunition pouch beside him.[17]

It was remarkable that the Pillar avoided being destroyed when so much of the surrounding street was reduced to rubble. For the defeated, it was disappointing that Admiral Nelson's statue still dominated the Dublin skyline, but, on the plus side, Daniel O'Connell's statue also survived.

By the time Pearse read out the Proclamation, a green, white and gold tricolour had been hoisted above the GPO by Michael Staines, Quarter-master General of the Volunteers, alongside a standard of green poplin with a harp.[18] Later that day, James Connolly sent a message to his soldiers: 'For the first time in 700 years the flag of a free Ireland floats triumphantly in Dublin City.'[19]

The making of the 1916 flag was the responsibility of Seán Mac Diarmada, whose polio prevented him taking a more active role in the Rising. It was made from Irish linen, in the fashion of the French tricolour, with three sections or 'fields', coloured green, white and golden yellow. However, the drapers Mac Diarmada commissioned for the job bungled the order and got the colours muddled. When the twenty-nine by sixty-three inch flag arrived at the GPO, the three fields had to be hastily unstitched, rearranged and restitched. Mac Diarmada rejected the invoice.

The fate of the flag later became the subject of a rather interesting story. When the British forces stormed the GPO, the tricolour was reputedly

A clock on the wall of the GPO showing the hour
that it stopped in 1916.

scooped up by Sergeant Tommy Davis of the Royal Dublin Fusiliers, who
dispatched it to his home in Lisburn, Co. Antrim, for safe-keeping. Three
months later, Davis returned home from the Somme an invalid and was
placed in the care of a Dr George St George. In lieu of payment, Davis
gifted the flag to the doctor, who, upon his death in 1922, passed it on
to his son-in-law, Captain Samuel Waring, MC, of Kells, Co. Meath. In
1951 Captain Waring presented it to his neighbour William Sweetman,
the son of John Sweetman, co-founder and sometime president of Sinn
Féin. There is some debate about where the flag resides today. The American
Irish Historical Society claims it is held at its headquarters on Fifth Avenue
in New York, while Ireland's National Museum maintains that its slightly
singed tricolour is the true flag of the GPO.

One of two photographs taken by chemist and Red Cross Volunteer Joseph Cripps on Easter Tuesday. The five men from the left were Irish Volunteers (*left to right*): Des O'Reilly (B Company, 1st Battalion), James Mooney (E Company, 2nd Battalion), Paddy Byrne (1st Battalion), Jack Doyle and Sergeant Tom McGrath (C Company, 2nd Battalion). The young fellow sitting on the right has been named as Tony Swan. The two men standing on the right were Hugh Thornton (killed in the Civil War) and John Twamley of the ICA. On the day this photo was taken, Twamley led the party of Volunteers who built barricades across the road at Wynn's Hotel.

While we may sing of the 'green, white and gold', the idea that part of our national flag could be considered 'gold' was written out of the script by the authors of the Irish Constitution in 1937. Article 7 states: 'The national flag is the tricolour of green, white and orange'.

A post office may not seem like the most logical base for an insurrection. However, as well as being a vital communications hub, the early nineteenth-century GPO was considered a solid and relatively defensible structure, well suited to its adopted role as headquarters for the Rising's leaders. It was also in a central location, with good communication lines to the other republican positions within the city. Over the course of the week, at least 508 rebels were in the building at some point. An ingenious wire pulley system was set up from the GPO to the Imperial Hotel directly opposite, and messages in cans were sent back and forth, allowing easy communication with no exposure for the men, until it was destroyed later in the week. Moreover, by taking the GPO, the rebels severely hampered their opponent's communication system during the first part of Easter Week.

British reaction to the occupation of the GPO was slow and for the first part of the week the occupants saw little action. On Easter Monday they fired on a party of Lancers who came to investigate reports of the attack on the GPO. The soldiers quickly withdrew when they were fired on. However, the Volunteers knew the relative calm would not last. A plan was set in motion to create an escape route and by Wednesday evening the men had bored and sledge-hammered their way through a series of walls on Henry Street to reach the Coliseum Theatre which stood opposite the end of Moore Street. No doubt this precaution seemed sensible as the week drew on and the British forces increased the pressure. By Thursday the GPO was under heavy artillery bombardment and the British Army was slowly reclaiming the surrounding streets, cutting the building off from the other positions and from any possible reinforcements. With James Connolly, their military leader, seriously wounded, it soon became apparent to the GPO garrison that the end of the occupation was at hand.

At the end of the Rising the GPO building, which had only recently been refurbished, was utterly gutted by fire. Only the façade survived, but the building was restored during the early years of the Irish Free State and reopened for business in 1929. From 1928 until 1973, life in the GPO was much animated by the presence of Raidió Éireann, which aired from studios on the third and fourth floors of the Henry Street wing. The GPO continues to function as the headquarters of the Irish postal service to this day and includes an exhibit that offers visitors an insight into the history of this neoclassical giant at the heart of Dublin.

Among the Irish Volunteers who garrisoned the GPO during the Rising were Sergeant Tom McGrath (*right*) and Jack Doyle of C Company in the Dublin Brigade's 2nd Battalion. This is the second of two photographs taken on Easter Tuesday by Joseph Cripps, who spent the week working as a medic in the Sackville Street area. Sadly, he had only two exposures left on his camera roll and one can only imagine what other gems he might have snapped if he had had more.

The ruins of the GPO in the aftermath of the Rising.

Joseph Plunkett

Joseph Mary Plunkett, the youngest of the Proclamation signatories, came from a relatively prosperous background. He was born at 26 Upper Fitzwilliam Street on Dublin's south side, the eldest son of George Noble Plunkett, a papal count who was curator of the National Museum in Dublin at the time of the Rising. His mother was Josephine Cranny.

Joseph, known as Joe, contracted tuberculosis as a boy, which prompted his family to send him for long sojourns in the warmer climates of Sicily, Algeria and Egypt. His education was strong: the Catholic University School on Dublin's Leeson Street, secondary school with the Jesuits at Belvedere College and later at Stonyhurst College in Lancashire. He became a poet and joined the Gaelic

League. Rather less predictably, he was a fluent Esperanto speaker, co-founding the Irish Esperanto League in 1907. He also reputedly won the Algerian roller-skating championships in 1911.

In 1909 his mother hired Thomas MacDonagh as a tutor to help Joe pass his entrance examinations into UCD. The two formed a particularly tight friendship, bonded by a love of poetry, theatre, mischief and, later, the Gifford sisters; MacDonagh married Muriel Gifford in 1912 and his sister-in-law, Grace, would ultimately become Joe Plunkett's wife.

The Plunkett family became increasingly radical in the years before the Rising, with Joe and his brothers to the fore of the Irish Volunteers in 1913. Plunkett and MacDonagh were editors of *The Irish Review* when, in July of that year, it carried an article by Roger Casement presciently entitled 'Ireland, Germany and the Next War'. They both served on the Industrial Peace Committee devised by Tom Kettle to break the deadlock of the 1913 Lockout and they were also planning to establish a new theatre on Hard-wicke Street to rival the Abbey.

When the First World War began in Europe, Count Plunkett allowed a mill on his Larkfield property in Kimmage, south Dublin, to be used as a secret camp for Irish Volunteers who had come over from Glasgow, Liverpool and London to play their part in any imminent action. Joe and his brother George devoted much of their energy to training these men, who became known as the 'Kimmage Garrison'.

In 1915 Joe joined the IRB, and that May he was dispatched to Germany to help Casement secure German arms ahead of the impending rebellion. Much of the plan for the Easter Rising is said to have originated with Joe Plunkett. His sisters Philomena and Fiona were also closely involved. However, when the time came, the Plunketts' concept was instantly scuppered by the capture of Casement and the countermanding order issued by MacNeill.

On Easter Monday Captain George Plunkett waved down a tram with his revolver at Harold's Cross and ordered the Kimmage Garrison to board, complete with shotguns, pikes and home-made billy-can bombs. He then took out his wallet and rather brilliantly requested, 'Fifty-two tuppenny tickets to the city centre, please.'

Joe Plunkett was unable to participate in the Rising to any great extent due to an operation on his neck glands a few days before it began. However, he remained in the GPO for the week, assisted by a dynamic young aide-de-camp called Michael Collins.

Seven hours before he was executed by a firing squad in Kilmainham Gaol, the twenty-eight-year-old poet was married in the prison chapel to his sweetheart, Grace Gifford. His sister Geraldine later claimed that Grace was pregnant at the time but subsequently miscarried.

Joe Plunkett's office at his father's farmhouse at Larkfield in Kimmage in south Dublin, pictured following a raid by British intelligence officers in the wake of the Rising. The house had been the base of the 'Kimmage Garrison' established by Joe and his brother George.

Grace Gifford, dressed in the ensemble she wore at her wedding to Joe Plunkett just hours before his execution. The daughter of a wealthy, Catholic, unionist lawyer and his Protestant wife, Grace was raised as a Protestant and attended Alexandra College, a girl's school which was then located on Earlsfort Terrace in central Dublin. A talented caricaturist and artist, she went on to study at the Slade School of Art. By the time she met Plunkett, she had become deeply committed to the Irish cultural revival.

A PROCLAMATION

Regulations to be observed under
MARTIAL LAW

I, Major-General, the Right Hon. L. B. Friend, C.B., Commanding the Troops in Ireland hereby Command that

(1) All persons in Dublin City and County shall keep within their houses between the hours of 7.30 p.m. in the evening and 5.30 a.m. on the next morning, on all days till further notice: unless provided with the written permission of the Military Authorities; or, unless in the case of fully qualified medical practitioners or medical nurses in uniform in the discharge of urgent duties.

(2) All persons other than members of His Majesty's Forces or Police, or acting in aid of said forces, who are seen carrying arms, are liable to be fired upon by the military without warning.

(3) All persons shall give all information in their possession as to stores of arms, ammunition, or explosives, or of the movement of hostile bodies to the nearest military authority, or to the nearest police barracks.

(4) All well disposed persons are hereby warned and advised to keep away from the vicinity of all places where military operations are in progress, or where hostile bodies are moving, and persons that enter such areas do so at their own risk.

Dated at Headquarters, Irish Command,

Park Gate, Dublin, 26th April, 1916

On Wednesday 26 April, approximately forty-eight hours after the rebellion broke out, Major General L. B. Friend, commander of British troops in Ireland, issued a Proclamation of Martial Law in Dublin city and county, including a curfew from 7.30 p.m. to 5.30 a.m., until further notice. This version comes from a contemporary album compiled by J. J. Simington, manager of *The Irish Times*.

Willie Pearse

Willie Pearse, the younger and only full brother of Patrick, was one of the dandiest men to participate in the Rising, being from a Bohemian circle of thespians and artists. A quiet, introspective boy, he became an exceptionally talented artist and sculptor, studying under Oliver Sheppard at the Dublin Metropolitan School of Art in Kildare Street, as well as in London and Paris.

Following his father's death, Willie found himself increasingly occupied sculpting altars and ecclesiastical works, such as the rather prophetic *Mater Dolorosa* at St Andrew's Church in Westland Row.

In 1914 Willie received a considerable blow when Mabel Gorman, his teenage muse, succumbed to tuberculosis. At that time, he was assisting his brother at Scoil Éanna, where he taught art, drawing and drama. He was also involved in staging an acclaimed Irish-language version of the Passion of Christ at the Abbey Theatre.

Having served as his brother's deputy headmaster at Scoil Éanna, Willie went on to serve as his deputy in the GPO. The precise reasons why he was marked out for execution in the aftermath of the Rising are unknown, but it is difficult not to conclude that he was executed simply because he was Patrick Pearse's brother.

Above: The east side of Sackville Street as seen from O'Connell Bridge, taken from *Dublin After the Six Days' Insurrection* by T. W. Murphy. Rather miraculously, John Henry Foley's mighty statue of Daniel O'Connell, to the left of the picture, survived all the artillery fire intact. Most of the damage to Sackville Street was caused by fire, particularly at the *Irish Times*' warehouse and Hoyte's Druggists and Oil Works, rather than by shelling.

Right top : Metal debris and bullet cartridges found in the GPO.

Right bottom: With the destruction at the GPO, temporary arrangements had to be made for Dublin's post. This photo shows a temporary sorting office set up in the Rotunda complex.

Arthur 'Boss' Shields

Arthur 'Boss' Shields, one of the greatest Irish actors of his generation, also served in the GPO during the Rising. His father, Adolphus Shields, a prominent Dublin socialist intellectual, was credited with introducing the Gas Workers' Union to Ireland. Arthur's mother, Fanny Ungerland, was a well-to-do German who had abandoned her home in Hamburg in protest at the unequal treatment of women in the family.

The Shields had eight children, and all were destined for creative careers. Arthur, their seventh child, was born on North Great

George's Street, Dublin, in 1896. In 1913 he began taking evening acting classes at the Abbey Theatre while working with Maunsel & Co. publishing company. His life took a dramatic turn in July 1914 when, just days before the outbreak of the First World War, he witnessed the moment when some soldiers from the King's Own Scottish Borderers opened fire on a crowd at Bachelor's Walk, leaving four dead. Outraged, he joined the Irish Volunteers and was given a rifle, which he secreted under the floorboards of the Abbey.

When the Easter Rebellion erupted, two years later, Arthur cycled straight to the Abbey to get his rifle. He reported to Liberty Hall, where he was greeted by James Connolly, who said, 'if you're as good a man as your father, you'll be all right'.[20] He spent the remainder of the week in and around the GPO before he and his fellow rebels surrendered on Moore Street.

Shields was sent to the internment camp at Frongoch in Wales. At a subsequent enquiry, the presiding magistrate recognised him as an actor he had seen in the Abbey, ordered him released and told him to go home, stick to theatre and 'forget about this revolutionary nonsense'.[21]

He returned to the Abbey, rising to become its most influential star, and later moved to Hollywood where, along with his brother Will (aka 'Barry Fitzgerald'), he enjoyed a successful career as a supporting actor and befriended John Wayne, Henry Fonda and James Cagney.

A crowd of mostly women line up outside the Dublin Savings Bank on Lower Abbey Street during the Rising.

Above: Dependants of soldiers in the British Army waiting for old age and separation allowances at the Aungier Street Post Office. The disruption to services greatly angered many of Dublin's citizens during the Rising, especially those whose sons, brothers and husbands were serving in the First World War.

Overleaf: Henry Street after the rebellion, taken from Nelson's Pillar.

British soldiers with guns at the ready stand amid the ruins of Henry Street with Nelson's Pillar towering behind them. At the right of the picture, the bombed-out Coliseum Theatre can be identified by the canopy over the door.

Top: The interior of the Hotel Metropole, which stood beside the GPO. This was the hotel where Joe Plunkett was recuperating over the Easter weekend immediately before the Rising. Within a week, almost nothing of it remained.

Bottom: The corner of Bachelor's Walk and Sackville Street.

Based at 34 Henry Street, the premises of Dundon &
Co., Tailors, Hatters and Outfitters, was utterly destroyed
during the Rising, along with most of that side of the street.
Rather a pity if you happened to have left your trousers in
with them to have the girth loosened that particular week.
The photograph was taken by John Chancellor, whose
studio stood nearby.

157

LIBERTY HALL AND HMS *HELGA*

On Easter Monday the Royal Navy dispatched HMS *Helga* from her base in Kingstown (present-day Dún Laoghaire) to the River Liffey. *Helga's* early years had been rather sedate. Built in a Dublin dockyard for the Department of Agriculture in 1908, she was initially used for fishery patrols and scientific research, including the survey of Clare Island, Co. Mayo, from 1909 to 1911. In 1915 she was pressed into war service and classified as an 'armed auxiliary patrol yacht'. On her bow were two quick-firing 12-pounder coastal defence guns, with a range of 11,000 metres and a firing rate of fifteen rounds per minute. Three smaller 3-pound 'pompom' guns were also installed at the stern. Before the Rising, *Helga* served as an anti-submarine patrol and escort vessel.

On Easter Tuesday *Helga* sent some salvos into Boland's Mill before heading to the electric power station at the Pigeon House which was apparently due to be attacked. When the Pigeon House was secured, *Helga* returned back upriver. At 8 a.m. on Wednesday morning she opened fire on Liberty Hall, directing her shells under the viaduct of the Loopline Bridge rather than over it as sometimes claimed.[22]

Liberty Hall, formerly the Northumberland Hotel, was the headquarters of the ICA and the ITGWU. In October 1914 James Connolly had hung a banner on the exterior of the building which declared 'We serve neither King nor Kaiser but Ireland.' Before the rebellion, it had been a covert munitions factory where bombs and bayonets were manufactured, as well as first-aid kits and knapsacks for the soldiers of the ICA.[23]

On Easter Sunday all the signatories to the Proclamation except Plunkett, who was in hospital, met there to discuss the situation following Mac-Neill's countermand. The following morning nearly 1,000 men and women from the Irish Volunteers, the ICA and Cumann na mBan assembled outside the building before marching on the GPO.

Liberty Hall was left largely undefended but was destroyed on the Wednesday by a combination of shells fired from *Helga* and from Howitzers based at Trinity College Dublin. The twenty-four-round bombardment from *Helga* destroyed the entire north section of Liberty Hall, as well as the adjoining Northumberland House. It is not clear whether the assailants thought the building was occupied or whether its destruction was intended to crush the morale of the rebel army.

Helga was inherited by the Irish Department of Agriculture and Fisheries in 1923. Renamed the *Muirchu* (*Seahound*), she was wrecked off Tuskar Rock in 1947 en route to be broken up by the Hammond Lane Foundry in Dublin.[24] Liberty Hall was faithfully reconstructed in the years after the Rising, but was later replaced by the present-day sixteen-storey tower built between 1961 and 1965. A statue of Connolly stands beneath the Loopline facing Liberty Hall.

HMS *Helga*.

The ruins of Liberty Hall, headquarters of the ITGWU and the ICA, following the Rising.

James Connolly

James Connolly has been variously described 'as one of the most dangerous revolutionaries in Europe' and 'probably the most important political thinker' in early twentieth-century Ireland.[25] Even though he spoke with a Scottish accent and was born and raised in the slums of Edinburgh, he always felt a closer bond to Ireland than Scotland. (Both his parents were Irish Catholics who are thought to have emigrated from near Clones in west Monaghan about a decade before his birth in 1868.)

After a spell as a bakers' apprentice, fourteen-year-old Connolly lied about his age and joined the British Army, enlisting in the 1st

Battalion of the King's Liverpool Regiment. In 1882 the battalion was posted to Ireland, where it remained until 1889. During this time he met Lillie Reynolds, a Protestant from Carnew, Co. Wicklow, who was working as a domestic servant for a family called Wilson in Dublin. Connolly left the army in 1889, and the following year he and Lillie were married in Perth.

Connolly was working as a manure carter for the Edinburgh Cleansing Department when he joined the socialist movement. By 1895 he was secretary of the Scottish Socialist Federation. He moved to Dublin to become full-time secretary to the Dublin Socialist Club, which he disbanded to form the Irish Socialist Republican Party. Over the next seven years he established himself as one of the pre-eminent Marxist theorists in the United Kingdom, founding the Socialist Labour Party in 1903.

He left Dublin for the USA that same year, and over the next seven years he became actively involved in the socialist movement across America. In 1910 he returned to Ireland and was appointed Ulster organiser for Jim Larkin's ITGWU. In 1912 he co-founded the Irish Labour Party as the ITGWU's political wing. Together with ex-British officer Jack White, he also co-founded the ICA to help workers defend themselves against police brutality.

Initially somewhat scornful of the Irish Volunteers, Connolly agreed to join their insurrection following a series of meetings with the IRB's Military Council in 1916.

His daughter Nora recalled meeting him shortly after he had learned about MacNeill's countermand. 'Daddy ... What does it mean? Why are we not going to fight?' she asked. 'He sat up in the bed. The tears ran down his face. ... He said, "The only thing we can do is to pray for an earthquake to come and swallow us and our shame."'[26]

During the Rising, Connolly was Commandant General of the Dublin Brigade at the GPO. Fatally wounded in the fighting, he was taken prisoner after the surrender and brought to a temporary hospital ward at the State Apartments in Dublin Castle. On 12 May he was carried into Kilmainham Gaol on a stretcher. After he was given absolution and the last rites by a Capuchin friar, Father Aloysius, he was tied to a chair and shot by a firing squad.

Major E. H. Heathcote of the 6/7 Sherwood Foresters personally oversaw at least seven of the executions, including Connolly's. From what he later told Robert Barton, Connolly 'was probably drugged and … almost dead' when they shot him. 'He was not able to sit upright in the chair on which he was placed,' Barton stated, 'and, when they shot him, the whole back of the chair was blown out.'[27]

THE FOUR COURTS AND NORTH KING STREET

During the Rising, the Four Courts and surrounding areas were occupied by the 1st Battalion of the Dublin Brigade, Irish Volunteers, commanded by Ned Daly. Their objective was to prevent reinforcements from the military barracks in Phoenix Park and the west of the city reaching the GPO. Daly's headquarters were at the Father Mathew Hall in Church Street. Although his battalion initially numbered just 150 men, the ranks were swelled by new arrivals throughout the week. To secure their position, they barricaded the surrounding streets and fortified a series of strategic outposts, most famously at Reilly's pub, nicknamed Reilly's Fort and now called 'The Tap', on the corner of Church Street and North King Street. The premises were filled with sacks of flour and meal taken from the near-by Blanchardstown Mills. Daly also positioned snipers on the rooftops of the Four Courts and Jameson's Malthouse to provide extra protection. By this means, he gained control of all three streets leading down to the Four Courts itself.

On Easter Monday Daly's men overpowered a force of Lancers, providing one of the first morale-boosters for the rebel cause. Two days later they captured the Bridewell police station. Possibly acting on Connolly's orders, they also set fire to the Linenhall Barracks, which was occupied by unarmed army clerks.

Fighting intensified from Thursday, when soldiers from the South Staffordshire and Sherwood Forest regiments cordoned off the area and began 'mouse-holing' through the walls of the surrounding tenements, house to house. One of the more insane moments of the rebellion occurred when Lieutenant James Sheppard of the South Staffordshires led his platoon on a suicidal bayonet charge at one of Daly's barricades. Fifteen men fell, Sheppard was wounded. A civilian medical officer who came to administer first aid was also killed.

It took the British forces two days to capture less than 140 metres of North King Street, at a cost of eleven dead and thirty-two wounded. However, an improvised armoured car finally broke through on Friday, enabling the British to advance on foot behind it and take the rest of the street. That night, the South Staffordshires – young, scared, green, participating in their first action and already psychologically scarred – completely lost the run of themselves on North King Street. They seized, tortured and either shot or bayoneted fifteen male civilians to death. Colonel Taylor, who commanded the British forces, later claimed that 'no persons were attacked by the troops other than those who were assisting the rebels or who had arms in their possession'.[28]

The subsequent military inquest was headed up by Colonel Ernest Maconchy, the commander of the Sherwood Foresters, who had lost so many men at Mount Street Bridge. No action was taken against Colonel Taylor or his men. That the dead men were unarmed civilians was not questioned, but the inquest preferred to follow the lead of General Maxwell, commander of the British forces in Ireland, who stated, 'It is perfectly possible that some were innocent but they could have left their houses if they so wished and the number of such incidents that have been brought to notice is happily few … Under the circumstance the troops as a whole behaved with the greatest restraint.'[29] The findings of the inquest were not disclosed until 2001 for fear of hostile propaganda, but, in the weeks that followed the Rising, the massacre on North King Street was one of the events that turned popular opinion strongly against the British forces.

Damage to the Four Courts sustained during the Rising.

At 3.05 a.m. on Friday, the Dublin Fire Brigade responded to a call to attend to a raging fire on Usher's Quay on the southern banks of the River Liffey. The fire destroyed H. Kavanagh's Wine & Spirit Merchant, as well as the premises of the Dublin Clothing Company factory next door and a tramcar and a street barricade. It also spread into buildings on Lower Bridge Street including Doherty's Hotel, a tenement house and the Brazen Head Hotel. Kavanagh's had been occupied by soldiers from the Royal Dublin Fusiliers, who were firing across the river at Ned Daly's garrison in the Four Courts. Under heavy fire, Peadar Clancy and Tom Smart from Daly's garrison crossed the bridge with cans of petrol, broke into the ground floor of Kavanagh's and set the building alight. The two men then hightailed it back over the bridge and rejoined their garrison.[30]

Shortly before dawn on Saturday 29 April the Volunteers in Reilly's Fort were obliged to retreat to the Capuchin church on Church Street when they ran out of ammunition. That evening Nurse Elizabeth O'Farrell reached Daly with Pearse's order to surrender. As he passed the letter to his deputy, Piaras Béaslaí, Daly put his head in his hands and wept.

The remains of the fire on Usher's Quay set by Peadar Clancy and Tom Smart. The large four-storey building marked 'Liverpool, London & Lisbon' belonged to a shipping company and appears to have escaped the worst of the furnace. The cavalryman in this photograph is thought to have been a City of London Yeomanry Trooper (or Rough Rider) from the Phoenix Park Barracks. He carries a rifle, with his collar buttoned-up and no sleeve braid.

An improvised armoured personnel carrier outside the Granville Hotel (now the Savoy Cinema) on Sackville Street. Originally a flatbed truck, it was mounted with four boilers from the Guinness Brewery bolted together at the Inchicore Railway Works. This vehicle and others like it enabled troops to be brought into the heat of the battle with considerably less exposure to enemy fire. Holes drilled into the sides of the boilers enabled the occupants to poke their rifles out and return fire. Carriers like these were primarily used in the North King Street area.

Ned Daly

Edward (Ned) Daly, the twenty-five-year-old brother-in-law of Tom Clarke, was the youngest man to hold the rank of commandant during the Rising and the youngest to be executed in its aftermath. Born in Limerick city in 1891, he was the only boy in a family of eight sisters. Republicanism ran deeply through his blood. When his father, Edward, died of heart disease at the age of forty-one, six months before Ned's birth, the funeral occasioned one of the biggest gatherings of Irish nationalists in Limerick's history. The predominant reason Edward drew so many mourners was on account of his older brother John Daly, the Head Centre for the IRB in Connaught, who was serving a lifetime sentence at Chatham Prison in Kent for treason and dynamite offences.

After Edward's death, a fund was set up to provide for his family and his widow, Catherine, attempted to run a pub. In 1894 the Dalys were blessed with the return of James Daly, a brother of Edward and John, who had a made a fortune as a trader and sheep farmer on the French Pacific island of New Caledonia. He looked after the family until 1896 when John Daly was released from prison and moved in with the family. James was a supporter of constitutional nationalism and could not stomach his brothers' hard-line belief that force was a justifiable means of attaining the nationalist objective.

By 1899 the garrulous, cigar-smoking, whiskey-drinking John Daly was the foremost nationalist in Limerick, serving three terms as the city's mayor. In the years before the Rising he funded several nationalist newspapers as well as establishing the Limerick branch of the Irish Volunteers. Of most immediate relevance to the fate of his nephew Ned, he also played a key role in securing Tom Clarke's release from prison in 1898. When Clarke came to thank him, his eye lit upon John Daly's twenty-one-year-old niece Kathleen – one of Ned's older sisters. The couple were married in New York in 1901. Another frequent visitor to the house was Seán Mac Diarmada, who was adored by the Daly family.

All this made for an exciting childhood for Ned Daly although his education with the Presentation Sisters and the Christian Brothers in Limerick reveals nothing remarkable. In 1906 he spent a year at Leamy's School, learning the ropes of commerce, where a professor described him as 'a brilliant boy' but with 'no aptitude for study'.[31] The following year his uncle John sent him to Glasgow to master bakery, confectionery and breadmaking, but ultimately the Limerick Bakers' Society refused to admit him, probably because he was not the son of a baker.

Various stints as a clerk followed, but Ned was becoming ever more irascible, frequently arguing with his autocratic uncle John. Possessed of a fine baritone voice, Ned preferred the company of his friends with whom he listened to the music of McCormack and Caruso on a gramophone. John worried that Ned had become a 'mollycoddle' – 'his mother, I think, spoiled him and made a sissy of him'.[32]

Ned was anything but a 'sissy'. Much of his spare time was spent studying books and manuals on war and military strategy. In 1913, following a massive row with John Daly, Ned moved to Dublin. Based at Tom and Kathleen Clarke's house in Fairview, he went to work as a chemist's assistant on Westmoreland Street but found it so dull that he began to seriously contemplate emigration to the USA.

Things changed for him in November 1913, with the foundation of the Irish Volunteers. Already living at the heart of revolutionary Ireland, Ned was immediately drawn to the organisation. 'I never saw a happier young man than he was the night he joined,' wrote Kathleen. 'He told me it was what he had always been wishing for.'[33] Kathleen and another six of Ned's sisters later joined Cumann na mBan.

Ned joined B Company of the 1st Battalion as a private but quickly proved himself a born leader and was elected captain of B Company. His first lieutenant was his future best friend, Jim O'Sullivan, a twenty-two-year-old grocer's assistant. As the men beneath them were a good deal older than they were, the pair grew moustaches to add a sense of gravitas. Neither moustache was particularly impressive, but Ned's stern, unassuming and by-the-book demeanour won the respect of his men, as did his baritone when he belted out verse and chorus of 'Eileen Óg' on route marches; it duly became the regimental song of the 1st Battalion. His men performed with considerable aplomb during the Howth gun-running of 1914, during which Ned oversaw much of the military operation. He was promoted to the rank of commandant in March 1915.

At Ned Daly's trial, his claims that he was simply following orders were rejected. He was executed by firing squad on 4 May.

Opposite: The front page of the *Excelsior*, a daily French illustrated newspaper, dated 5 May 1916, depicting images of the Rising.

SEPTIÈME ANNÉE. — N° 1998.   LE NUMÉRO: 10 CENTIMES. — ÉTRANGER: 20 CENTIMES   Vendredi 5 mai 1916.

·EXCELSIOR·

Journal Illustré Quotidien

Informations - Littérature - Sciences - Arts - Sports - Théâtres - Élégances

LA RÉVOLTE DE DUBLIN EST RÉPRIMÉE

EARL STREET

BOUTIQUES PILLÉES PAR LES REBELLES

SACKVILLE STREET

Gal MAXWELL

Csse MARKIEWICZ

ABLE SHOE CO. L.

MAGASIN PILLÉ PAR LES REBELLES

MAISONS DE SACKVILLE STREET EN RUINES

Le calme est absolument rétabli dans Dublin. Les chefs de la révolte sont tombés aux mains des troupes britanniques, et parmi eux la comtesse Markiewicz. Le général Maxwell commandait les régiments qui, par une énergique action, ont rétabli l'ordre. Divers quartiers ont assez gravement souffert, notamment la Sackville-Street, où de nombreuses maisons ont été ruinées par l'incendie.

MENDICITY INSTITUTION:
HEUSTON'S FORT

During the Rising, acting under direct orders from James Connolly, Captain Seán Heuston's unit occupied the Mendicity Institution on the south bank of the River Liffey. The charitable institution was based at Moira House on Usher Island, the same building where Lady Pamela FitzGerald had learned of the death of her husband, Lord Edward, during the 1798 Rebellion twelve decades earlier.

Heuston's small force of twenty-six young Volunteers, including Fianna stalwarts Paddy Joe Stephenson, Seán McLoughlin, Liam Staines and Dick Balfe, had been instructed by Connolly to hold up any troops moving towards the Four Courts in order to allow Ned Daly's garrison to establish itself properly.

On Easter Monday they quickly moved in, removing its occupants at gunpoint and barricading the windows with whatever they could find. McLoughlin, with the help of some press-ganged members of the public, erected a barrier across Bridge Street. It was anticipated that they would stay at the Mendicity for no more than four hours, but Heuston's young men actually held the post for over fifty hours, despite being subjected to 'the singing bullets and the rattle-rattle of the barking, hammering, persistent machine guns', as Stephenson recalled it.[34]

On Wednesday the building came under fierce attack from the Royal Dublin Fusiliers. When the soldiers began hurling grenades through the windows, the men within did what they could to scoop them up and throw them out again – two Volunteers died in the process and Staines and Balfe were injured. Realising the hopelessness of their situation, and eager to get the wounded to hospital as quickly as possible, Heuston hoisted the white flag of surrender on Wednesday afternoon.[35]

'Whatever I have done, I have done as a soldier of Ireland, and I have no regrets,' wrote the twenty-five-year-old shortly before he was executed at Kilmainham Gaol on 8 May at 3.45 a.m. Kingsbridge Railway Station was renamed Heuston Station in his honour.

Seán Houston

Born in Dublin in 1891, Seán Heuston moved to Limerick city at the age of seventeen to work for the Great Southern and Western Railway. In 1911 the twenty-year-old was instrumental in establishing the Limerick branch of Fianna Éireann in a hall at the back of John Daly's townhouse on Barrington Street. Within a year, the Barrington Hall sluagh was one of the largest Fianna branches in Ireland, and much of this success was credited to the quiet but effective Heuston.

In 1913 he returned to Dublin to work at Fianna headquarters and to take command of the Fianna sluagh at Hardwicke Street. He also joined the Irish Volunteers and became captain of 'D' Company in the 1st Battalion. The following year he played a prominent role in the Howth gun-running. When the Fianna organisation was restructured in 1915, Heuston was appointed to the National Fianna Executive and became Director of Training, as well as vice-commandant of the Fianna Dublin Brigade.

Heuston was court-martialled on 4 May 1916. One piece of evidence used against him was the written order from Connolly to take the Mendicity Institution. Heuston unsuccessfully attempted to defend himself on the grounds that the name in the order was spelt Houston, and therefore could not be taken to mean him.

Fr Albert Bibby (*left*) with Fr Dominic O'Connor on Church Street. Fr Bibby, OFM Capuchin, was the monk who attended Seán Heuston before his execution in Kilmainham Gaol. After the final volley of shots rang out, he observed the dead man's face and found it 'transformed, and lit with a grandeur and brightness I had never before noticed'.[36]

The Royal Dublin Fusiliers

A Royal Dublin Fusiliers recruitment parade in 1915.

During the First World War, thousands of Irishmen enlisted in the Royal Dublin Fusiliers. The 4th, 5th and 10th Battalions were involved in the Rising; twelve of their members were killed and at least thirty-two were wounded. John Dillon, deputy leader of the IPP, subsequently recalled asking General Maxwell, 'Have you any cause of complaint of the Dublins [the Royal Dublin Fusiliers] who had to go down and fight their own people in the streets of Dublin? Did a single man turn back and betray the uniform he wears?' To which Maxwell replied, 'Not a man.'[37]

JACOB'S BISCUIT FACTORY

Approximately 150 members of Thomas MacDonagh's 2nd Battalion, Dublin Brigade, Irish Volunteers, assembled at St Stephen's Green shortly before midday on Easter Monday. MacDonagh briefly toyed with the idea of attacking Trinity College but ultimately he marched the main body of his men to Jacob's biscuit factory on Bishop Street, where the National Archives now stands. His orders were to hold the factory and establish outposts in the vicinity in order to stop British soldiers reaching the city centre from the nearby Portobello Barracks.

Built in the 1850s, Jacob's biscuit factory had been on the frontline of Dublin's protest since 1911, when the men in the bakehouse went on strike, prompted by Jim Larkin's assertion that the conditions were 'sending them from this earth twenty years before their time'.[38] Larkin's words came despite the fact that the Quaker-owned business offered its employees some of the best working conditions in Dublin at the time. Jacob's was also the largest employer of women in Dublin city in 1911, and the factory came to a standstill when 3,000 of its female employees – including a young Rosie Hackett – embarked on a sympathy strike in support of the men.

Two years later, Jacob's was back in the firing line when Larkin described it as 'the worst sweating den in Europe' in a pamphlet called 'Larkin's Scathing Indictment of Dublin Sweaters'. Jacob's successfully sued the publishers for libel and invited a number of prominent people to inspect the factory for themselves. During the 1913 strike and Lockout, Jacob's dismissed some 300 of its female employees for refusing to remove their union badges.

Among those who joined MacDonagh's battalion was Major John MacBride, whose considerable military experience compelled MacDonagh to appoint him as his second-in-command in lieu of his friend Michael O'Hanrahan. MacDonagh's men seized and barricaded the factory in the early afternoon. Every available vessel was filled with water in case the city's water supply was cut off.

Jacob's actually saw relatively little fighting during the week, with Brigadier General W. H. M. Lowe, commander of the British forces in Dublin prior to the arrival of General Maxwell, opting to concentrate on the GPO and the Four Courts, which he considered the more strategically important positions held by the insurgents. There may also have been concerns about possible damage to the nearby St Patrick's Cathedral, the national Church of Ireland cathedral.

An artist's impression of Jacob's biscuit factory.

Fr Augustine Hayden, one of the two Capuchin priests who persuaded MacDonagh's battalion to surrender.

As such, MacDonagh's men spent the week in mounting anxiety, isolated from the other battalions and operating on the increasingly infrequent updates from the garrison on St Stephen's Green. Otherwise, they could only speculate about what was going on as they listened to the distant shells and gunfire and watched the smoke billowing from the city centre. They also had to contend with considerable abuse from women living in the locality, who were incensed that the city had been brought to a standstill.

Awaiting an assault that never came, they were bitterly dismayed when Fr Aloysius Travers and Fr Augustine Hayden, two Capuchin priests, brought news of Pearse's order to stand down on Sunday afternoon. The priests urged MacDonagh to surrender, advising him of Lowe's warning that failure to do so would compel him 'to attack and demolish the factory with great loss of life'.[39] Fr Hayden was also instrumental in securing the surrender of Éamonn Ceannt's battalion at the South Dublin Union, and he administered last rites to both Ceannt and Con Colbert before their execution.

Fierce debates raged inside Jacob's, but, at length, MacDonagh told his men, 'We have to give in. Those of you who are in civilian clothes, go home. Those of you in uniform, stay on; you cannot leave.'[40] While some of those in civilian clothes chose to leave, many stayed to face the consequences. MacDonagh was one of several men who wept, while others furiously broke their rifles and revolvers on the ground, saying that they had been duped for nothing. The battalion's three most senior officers, MacDonagh, MacBride and Michael O'Hanrahan, were executed the following week.

In an interesting postscript to the story of Jacob's, Thomas W. Bewley, secretary at Jacob's, later wrote to Fr Aloysius. His letter was accompanied by a cheque for £25 from the directors of Jacob's to the Capuchins as a mark of appreciation for the 'deep sense of thankfulness that our Factory was spared from serious injury during the time of the recent rebellion'. Fr Aloysius returned the cheque, claiming that 'any services that I may have rendered during the recent sad crisis were such as … any other priest in the same circumstances would render'. He requested that the cheque be sent to the Lord Mayor's Fund for the Relief of Distress.

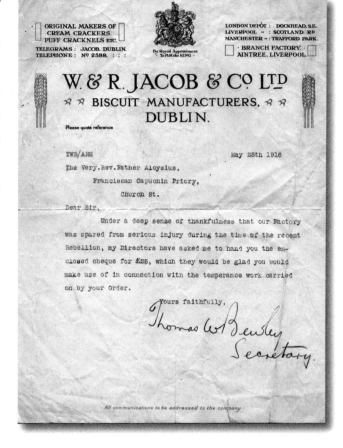

The letter from Thomas W. Bewley to Fr Aloysius.

Thomas MacDonagh

Born in Cloughjordan, Co. Tipperary, Thomas MacDonagh was the son of two teachers and was himself to become a teacher of much renown. His childhood was a creative one, rich in music, art, poetry and language. Narrowly avoiding a career as a missionary, he became a poet in his late teens and taught in Fermoy, Co. Cork, and later in Kilkenny College.

He moved to Dublin in 1908, befriended Eoin MacNeill and reconnected with Patrick Pearse, whom he had first met on a visit to the Aran Islands. The latter gave him a job teaching French and English at Scoil Éanna, as well as making him assistant headmaster. In 1909 MacDonagh was hired as tutor to Joe Plunkett, who became his greatest friend.

MacDonagh had an attractive personality, and Plunkett was not the only one who enjoyed his cheerful ramblings and strong sense of humour. In 1912 he married Muriel Gifford, who was working as a volunteer nurse in Dublin's inner-city slums. Later that year, he accepted a job as a lecturer in English history at UCD.

Following the formation of the Irish Volunteers, he was appointed commandant of Dublin's 2nd Battalion, later taking command of the entire Dublin Brigade. His organisational expertise came to the fore when he planned O'Donovan Rossa's funeral, where Pearse delivered his famous graveside oration.

As MacDonagh was not co-opted onto the IRB's secret Military Council until April 1916, it is assumed that he had little role in the conception or planning of the Rising. Nonetheless, he was a signatory to the Proclamation. He spent the week commanding the brigade at Jacob's, which saw relatively little action. Despite this he is said to have 'sobbed bitterly' when the order to surrender came through.[41]

On 3 May the thirty-eight-year-old was marched into the yard at Kilmainham Gaol and executed. 'I know this is a lousy job,' he said to the firing squad, 'but you're doing your duty – I do not hold this against you.'[42] A British officer who witnessed the execution remarked, 'they all died well but MacDonagh died like a Prince'.[43] His death prompted the poet Francis Ledwidge to pen his 'Lament for Thomas MacDonagh'.

MacDonagh's widow, Muriel, died of heart failure while swimming near Skerries in the summer of 1917. Their son, Donagh MacDonagh, became a judge, poet, Broadway playwright, songwriter and broadcaster.

Wives of the Proclamation signatories: Áine Ceannt (*top*) and Muriel MacDonagh (*bottom*).

Major John MacBride

Major John MacBride, who served as Thomas MacDonagh's impromptu second-in-command, was one of the most experienced soldiers to line out for the Irish Volunteers. He was born in 1865 in Westport, Co. Mayo, from where his father operated a merchant ship that sailed between the quay in Westport and MacBride's ancestral homeland in Co. Antrim.[44]

In his younger years, MacBride worked variously in a drapery shop in Castlerea, Co. Roscommon, and in a chemist's firm in Dublin. He took the Fenian oath at the age of fifteen and, by his early twenties, the hard-drinking redhead had joined both the IRB and the GAA. He also became a close friend of Sinn Féin founder Arthur Griffith, through the Celtic Literary Society.

In 1896 MacBride moved to South Africa to work in the gold mines, convincing Griffith to follow him out. When the Anglo-Boer War broke out, he raised the Irish Transvaal Brigade, later known as MacBride's Brigade, comprising some 500 Irish and Irish-Americans prepared to fight for the Boers against the British. MacBride was commissioned with the rank of major in the Boer Army and given Boer citizenship.

His support for the Boers also formed the basis of his initial relationship with the actress Maud Gonne, who, tiring of her letter-writing suitor W. B. Yeats, opted for this man of action instead. MacBride and Gonne went on a lecture tour across the USA in 1902 and married in Paris in 1903. They spent their honeymoon in Spain, during which time they conspired to assassinate Edward VII, who was visiting Gibraltar. The plot appears to have unravelled because MacBride went drinking with friends instead, prompting a massive bust-up between the newly-weds.[45] The marriage collapsed soon after the birth of their son, Seán, the following year; Maud accused him of violence, drunkenness and adultery.

MacBride returned to Dublin in 1905 and found work writing for *The Freeman's Journal*. He continued to support the nationalist cause, becoming a member of the IRB's Supreme Council in 1911. However, he was soon ejected in a purge and replaced by Seán Mac Diarmada.

He was not aware of the Rising until Easter Monday when, according to his own words at his court martial, he chanced to encounter 'a band of Irish Volunteers' on St Stephen's Green while waiting to lunch with his brother Anthony in Wicklow Street. Anthony was to be married two days later and had asked MacBride to stand as his best man. The Volunteers he saw were Thomas MacDonagh's men. In blue suit and white spats, a malacca cane at his side, MacBride sized up the situation and marched off with MacDonagh to Jacob's. And, as he explained at his court martial, 'after being a few hours there I was appointed second in command'.[46]

He was shot by firing squad two days before his forty-eighth birthday. MacBride was selected for execution largely because of his actions in the Anglo-Boer War. He refused to wear a blindfold, telling the firing squad, 'Fire away, I've been looking down the barrels of rifles all my life.' Tom Kettle proposed that MacBride had meant to say that 'he had been looking down the necks of porter bottles all his life'.[47] The Irish-American lawyer John Quinn, a close confidant of Maud Gonne, suggested that the firing squad was 'the best end possible for MacBride, a better end than … going on living in the past and drinking and talking out his life'.[48]

Seán MacBride, the only child of John and Maud, became a prominent human-rights activist, co-founding Amnesty International in 1961. He received the Nobel Peace Prize in 1974.

Marsh's Library

Marsh's Library, a well-preserved library of the late Renaissance and early Enlightenment, is located in the heart of the south inner city, across the road from the insurgent position at Jacob's. It also shared a boundary wall with the police station at Kevin Street. The only damage to the library came on Sunday 30 April, the day MacDonagh's battalion reluctantly surrendered, when a British Army machine-gunner located in the nearby Iveagh Buildings 'inadvertently' fired upon the library, apparently believing he had sighted a sniper in one of the windows. Significant damage was caused to the roof and windows on the north-facing side of the library, while the bullets also struck a bookshelf, 'injuring five books'. The shattered books provide an inkling of the effect of a bullet on frail human flesh and bone.[49]

The picture shows the damage done to Jean Mestrezat's religious tract *Traité de l'église* (Geneva, 1649).

Michael O'Hanrahan

Michael O'Hanrahan was born in New Ross, Co. Wexford, in 1877, a decade after his father, Richard, participated in the short-lived Fenian Rising. Shortly after Michael's birth, the family moved to Carlow town, where Richard ran a cork-cutting business on Tullow Street. In 1899 Michael and his brother Harry founded the Carlow branch of the Gaelic League, one of the first branches outside Dublin. Michael also co-founded the Carlow Workman's Club but left in protest when the club admitted a British soldier. During this time he adopted the Irish form of his name: Micheál Ó hAnnracháin.

In about 1902 the family moved to Dublin, where, after the premature death of Richard, they gave up cork-cutting and opened a tobacconist shop at 67 Connaught Street in Phibsborough, north

Dublin. Michael arrived in the city in time to assist Maud Gonne and Arthur Griffith in their campaign against Edward VII's visit to Ireland. In 1905 he was among the younger generation who, disillusioned with the IPP, joined the newly founded Sinn Féin political party. Arthur Griffith's ambitions for Irish economic independence appealed to the O'Hanrahans; Michael's sisters, Áine (Ciss), Máire and Eily, were likewise impressed by the party's willingness to offer women a role in politics.

Michael found work as a proof-reader for the Gaelic League printer An Cló Cumann. Together with Harry, he organised a major League excursion to Tara, Co. Meath, in 1905, enjoyed by thousands, with games, music and refreshments.[50] He also wrote a number of journalistic articles and two well-regarded novels, *A Swordsman of the Brigade* and *When the Normans Came*, in which the heroes were brave Irishmen.

Almost certainly a member of the IRB, Michael was one of the first to join the Irish Volunteers when it was founded in 1913. He initially served as secretary and then as quartermaster to the 2nd Battalion, Dublin Brigade, under his close friend and literary colleague Thomas MacDonagh. After the split with Redmond's National Volunteers, he worked in the Irish Volunteers' headquarters at 2 Dawson Street, helping to rebuild the organisation. He became Quartermaster General of the Irish Volunteers in the months before the Rising.

During the Rising, O'Hanrahan was badly injured when he fell down a flight of stone steps inside Jacob's and concussed himself. He apparently played down the effects for fear that MacDonagh would send him to hospital. The thirty-nine-year-old was executed in Kilmainham Gaol on 4 May.[51]

THE SOUTH DUBLIN UNION

Éamonn Ceannt, one of the seven signatories to the Proclamation, commanded approximately 120 Volunteers from the 4th Battalion of the Dublin Brigade. They assembled at Emerald Square, Dolphin's Barn, on Easter Monday and marched to the twenty-hectare South Dublin Union (now St James's Hospital) off James's Street. 'This walled community,' wrote Charles Townshend, 'was the country's biggest poorhouse, with 3,000 destitute inmates, its own churches, stores, refectories, and two hospitals with full medical staff.'[52] As well as the multiple buildings, there was a large green space in the middle of the compound. Ceannt also assigned his men to several nearby outposts including the Watkin's Brewery, Roe's Distillery and the distillery on Marrowbone Lane.

Irrespective of the fact that over 3,000 luckless inmates and staff were inside when the Union was occupied, the position was strategically sound, placing the Volunteers near to both the Richmond Barracks in Inchicore and the Royal Hospital at Kilmainham, as well as allowing them to hinder British movements from Kingsbridge Railway Station.

Among those serving under Ceannt at the South Dublin Union were Volunteer Lieutenant W. T. Cosgrave and his two stepbrothers. Cosgrave, a Dublin publican, had been a reforming Sinn Féin councillor on Dublin Corporation since 1909. His family home was close to the South Dublin Union, and his good relations with the neighbouring community were useful for the delivery of food and messages.[53] Throughout the week, his mother could hear the gunfire from the building, knowing that three of her sons were involved. Her stepson, Frank 'Gobban' Burke, was actually shot dead by a sniper while lighting a cigarette on the Tuesday morning.[54]

The fighting for the South Dublin Union began on Monday afternoon, when the Volunteers fired on a Royal Irish Regiment picket that was attempting to reach the city centre. This led to a fierce assault on the Union in which several of the terrified inmates and a nurse were killed, and both sides of the combatants suffered heavy casualties. By midnight, British forces had regained control of the entire back side of the institution. However, Ceannt's men still held the buildings at the front, overlooking James's Street, and, despite repeated attacks by the superior armed British forces, they managed to retain them for the next six days.

W. T. Cosgrave, who went on to become the first president of the Executive Council of the Irish Free State from 1922 to 1932.

Cathal Brugha, Ceannt's second-in-command, was the hero of a particularly courageous action on the Thursday of Easter Week. Despite having been severely wounded by a hand grenade, he single-handedly held off an attack on his position in the Nurses' Home until Ceannt could bring up reinforcements. Indeed, so effective were the Volunteers in repulsing the assault that the British forces ceased trying to take the Union and instead resorted to pinning the rebels down for the remainder of the week.

On Sunday 30 April Thomas MacDonagh arrived at the South Dublin Union under a flag of truce, with Fr Augustine and Fr Aloysius. He informed Ceannt's garrison of Pearse's unconditional surrender. Grimly, Ceannt and Cosgrave accompanied Brigadier General Lowe to the rebel outpost in Marrowbone Lane where they conceded defeat. When Ceannt ordered the men in the Union to form up for surrender, only forty-one men of his original force were left to fall in. The British were surprised that such a small force had held them off so effectively.[55] Following the surrender, Cosgrave was taken to Richmond Barracks where he encountered William O'Brien, the trade-union leader. Cosgrave turned to O'Brien with a smile and observed, 'I imagine it will be a long time before we again discuss housing policy together.'[56]

The prisoners were marched to Bride Road in the company of Captain Auston Rotherham, an Olympic silver-medallist polo player from Co. Westmeath. The following day Rotherham was summoned to Richmond Barracks to give his testimony against the men. The court found him rather uncooperative. As Cosgrave recalled:

> His reply was that he had not seen these men yesterday, that he did not know them, not having seen them before, that he would not know them again; that he would not feel justified in giving testimony. It is but fair to say that his sight had become impaired, which was the reason assigned for his relinquishing polo.[57]

Cosgrave was lucky not to be executed. As he was a Sinn Féin councillor, the court assumed he was one of the ringleaders and sentenced him to death. This was later commuted to penal servitude for life by General Maxwell, in part because of his exemplary reputation in Dublin Corporation.

Éamonn Ceannt

Éamonn Ceannt (aka Edward Kent) was born in Ballymore, east Co. Galway, where his father was serving in the RIC. The family later moved to Ardee, Co. Louth, before settling in Dublin, where, like most of the Rising's leaders, Éamonn was educated by the Christian Brothers. He became both a musician and an athlete of considerable renown. Having mastered the uilleann pipes, bagpipes, flute, violin and tin whistle, he briefly, with his brothers, formed the Kent Brothers Band. Serious-minded, teetotal and an early adherent to the Gaelic League, Ceannt became a central figure in the revival of Irish traditional music, co-founding Cumann na bPíobairí (the Pipers' Club) in 1900.

In 1908 he was selected for a team of athletes who went to Rome, and his skills as an uilleann piper were employed to entertain Pope Pius X. Three years later he was sworn into the IRB by Seán Mac Diarmada. A natural military leader, he was one of the founding members of the Irish Volunteers in 1913 and commanded a section of Volunteers at the Howth gun-running in July 1914. He is also credited with convening a highly significant meeting at 25 Parnell Square, Dublin, in September 1914, at which leaders of the IRB, the Volunteers, the ICA and Sinn Féin agreed that England's war with Germany afforded a useful opportunity to strike a blow for Irish freedom.

Ceannt served on the Military Committee that planned the Rising, and during that tumultuous week he commanded over 100 Volunteers from the 4th Battalion, based at the South Dublin Union. He surrendered when called upon to do so by Pearse. The thirty-four-year-old musician was executed by firing squad in Kilmainham Gaol on 8 May 1916. In his final statement he wrote, 'Ireland has shown she is a nation. This generation can claim to have raised sons as brave as any that went before. And in the years to come, Ireland will honour those who risked all for her honour at Easter in 1916.'[58]

Ceannt's Dublin-born wife, Áine O'Brennan, served as vice-president of Cumann na mBan from 1917 to 1925. As an anti-Treaty activist she was jailed during the Civil War. She later co-founded the apolitical White Cross to assist families who had become impoverished during the War of Independence.

William Kent, brother of Éamonn, was a company sergeant major with the Royal Dublin Fusiliers. He was mortally wounded at Arras on 24 April 1917, exactly a year after the Rising began.

Con Colbert

Captain Con Colbert, the tenth of thirteen children, was born and raised in Co. Limerick. He moved to Ranelagh, south Dublin, in his early teens, attending school with the Christian Brothers on North Richmond Street.[59] In 1909 the twenty-one-year-old was present for the founding of Na Fianna Éireann and immediately became a chief scout in one of its city branches. He worked as a baker's clerk by day but increasingly devoted himself to the nationalist cause, particularly in recruiting boys to Fianna Éireann.

Colbert commanded a circle within the IRB that comprised Fianna like himself. He also acted as a drill instructor for the boys of Scoil Éanna. Elected onto the executive of the Irish Volunteers, he was made captain of F-Company in the 4th Battalion, Dublin Brigade. A young woman, Annie O'Brien, developed a deep crush on the Limerick man, but she was dismayed to find he was so 'engrossed in his work for Ireland' that he had no time for girls.[60]

On Easter Monday Colbert led the twenty men who seized Watkin's Brewery on Ardee Street on the south side of Dublin city, but, eager to get closer to the action, he transferred the unit to the nearby Jameson Distillery on Marrowbone Lane two days later, where he took over command. His decision to place a sniper in an open position close to the canal allowed the Volunteers to stop British soldiers attempting to enter the South Dublin Union via a back entrance. His men also managed to capture a bread van and some cattle, which helped bolster their food and drink supplies.[61] Colbert held the distillery until Sunday 30 April, when 'the gallant Captain Colbert', as Pearse called him, surrendered with the greatest reluctance.

Identified by G-Men, as Dublin Castle's detectives were known, Colbert was court-martialled and sentenced to death. Shortly before the guns fired, he pointed at the target pinned to his chest, a piece of white paper, saying 'wouldn't it be better to put it up nearer the heart'. His death became the subject of a powerful lament called 'Lovely Athea'. Limerick's railway station is named Colbert Station in his honour.[62]

TRINITY COLLEGE DUBLIN

Situated at the heart of Dublin city, Trinity College narrowly avoided a major attack by the 2nd Battalion of the Irish Volunteers when Thomas MacDonagh, the battalion's commandant, deemed the odds of high fatalities to be too great to risk. When word reached the college that a rebellion had begun, the porters swiftly locked the gates and ground-floor windows. John Gwynne, Regius Professor of Divinity at the university, sent the Trinity Rifle Club onto the roof of the college to discourage insurgents from trying to invade. The university, with its excellent vantage over Grafton Street, Nassau Street, College Green, College Street, Dame Street and Westmoreland Street, became a centre of operations against republican positions. Cadets from the Officer Training Corps (OTC) were soon posted to protect the college and began firing on rebel positions on Sackville Street. By Easter Tuesday, machine guns had been installed on the front parapet overlooking Dame Street and loyalist snipers occupied the rooftops.

During the Rising Trinity College served as a mustering base for British troops. Among those who assembled there were fourteen Dominion soldiers (six South Africans, five New Zealanders, two Canadians and an Australian) who happened to be on leave in Dublin when the Rising began. Each man was issued with a rifle from the OTC armoury and instructed to snipe the enemy.

Just after dawn on Easter Tuesday, Gerald Keogh, a twenty-year-old Volunteer dispatch rider from Ranelagh, was cycling at full pelt from St Stephen's Green towards the GPO when four OTC bullets slammed into

Above: British troops in Trinity College.

him just outside Trinity. Keogh was temporarily buried within the college grounds. Trinity also provided a temporary resting place for two British soldiers killed in the fighting. One of these was Private Arthur Charles Smith of the 4th Hussars, who was killed in action on 29 April. Private Smith, who hailed from Maldon, Essex, was initially buried at the foot of Trinity's boundary wall, where a stone plaque to his memory still survives. His remains were later removed to Grangegorman cemetery.

Future IRA leader Ernie O'Malley, who was studying medicine in Trinity, briefly toyed with the idea of assisting the OTC before he and a friend changed tack and began taking potshots at British soldiers. They were armed with a German Mauser rifle, which had been given to his friend's father as a present by a soldier who brought it back from the Western Front.[63]

After the Rising each member of the OTC who participated in the protection of the college was presented with a small silver cup engraved: 'DEFENCE OF T.C.D. – SINN FÉIN REBELLION – EASTER 1916'. Among the Defenders of Trinity College were Ernest Despard and Frederick Hoey, who both survived the Rising but were killed the following year; Despard while serving with the Tank Corps and Hoey in an air crash. Another was Frederic Nevin, a New Zealander from Christchurch, whose parents hailed from Co. Tipperary and Co. Cork respectively.

Right: The Defence of TCD Presentation Cup.

Left: General Sir John Grenfell Maxwell, commander of the British forces in Ireland, carries papers in his left hand as he inspects the veterans at Trinity College after the rebellion.

ST STEPHEN'S GREEN AND THE ROYAL COLLEGE OF SURGEONS

Michael Mallin in British Army uniform, India, *c.* 1899.

On Easter Monday Commandant Michael Mallin and a force of thirty-six soldiers from the ICA, supported by members of its Women's Section and a small number of Fianna Éireann, marched through the Fusiliers' Arch entrance into St Stephen's Green on the south side of Dublin city. Their primary objective was to occupy and hold the twenty-two-acre public park, which would give them control over a large section of traffic in the city centre. The 'Green' was also earmarked to serve as one of the rebels' principal bases should they successfully capture the city.

Commandant Mallin was second-in-command of the ICA under James Connolly. The son of a boatwright and carpenter from City Quay in Dublin's docklands, he enlisted in the 21st Royal Scots Fusiliers as a teenager, initially serving as a drummer boy in British India. His subsequent experiences during the Anglo-Boer War in South Africa turned him sharply against the British colonial system.

Upon leaving the army in 1902, the devout Catholic returned to Dublin, where he trained to become a silk-weaver. He also continued on with his music, both as a flautist and later as a band instructor with the ITGWU. He joined the Dublin Silk and Poplin Weavers' Trade Union, rising to become one of its leading spokesmen. Following the formation of the ICA, he became its chief training officer.

Captain Christopher (Kit) Poole, Mallin's deputy in the ICA, was placed in charge of operations in St Stephen's Green. Like Mallin, he had served in the British Army during the Anglo-Boer War.

Constance Markievicz commanded the women who served under Mallin in St Stephen's Green. By some accounts she eclipsed Kit Poole to become Mallin's second-in-command.[64] Increasingly frustrated as the week wore on, she once remarked that she longed for a bayonet or 'some stabbing instrument for action at close quarters', prompting Mallin to reply, 'You are very blood-thirsty.'[65]

Mallin's military training was to his benefit, and he was an immensely measured man. Critics suggest that he was strategically unimaginative, focusing too much attention on entrenching his forces in the Green, but he was undoubtedly stymied by having such a small force to work with. He did manage to establish a series of outposts in the area, most notably in the Royal College of Surgeons, but he failed to seize the Shelbourne Hotel that overlooked much of the Green's north side.

While Mallin's men were establishing themselves in the area on Easter Monday, thirteen civilians and British soldiers were shot. One of the two civilians who died was Michael Kavanagh, a thirty-four-year-old carter, who was killed when he tried to retrieve his cart from a barricade erected outside the Shelbourne. Also killed was Michael Lahiff, an unarmed twenty-eight-year-old constable of the Dublin Metropolitan Police. He was allegedly shot by Constance Markievicz, who is said to have run into the Green afterwards shouting 'I got him' in triumph.[66]

Early on Tuesday morning the Shelbourne was occupied by 120 British soldiers from Dublin Castle, who established a machine gun on the top floor. When the machine gun opened fire at 4 a.m., it proved so effective at slicing up the members of Mallin's garrison stationed in the Green that they were obliged to retreat into the Royal College of Surgeons, where they remained under siege for the rest of the week, surrounded by specimen jars and anatomical drawings and breathing in the formaldehyde fumes that saturated the air.

It had been envisioned that the St Stephen's Green garrison would be well placed to maintain communications with both Ceannt's men in Jacob's biscuit factory and de Valera's at Boland's Mill. However, aside from occasional contact with Jacob's, they were now largely isolated. All Mallin could do was organise his forces into a disciplined format and test out their marksmanship skills while they awaited developments from the GPO. Among his men was Rory O'Connor, destined to be executed during the Civil War, who was wounded by sniper fire during a reconnaissance mission from the college.

This garrison had a number of active women with them, whose main role was to organise first aid and food. These women, who included Nellie Gifford, Rosie Hackett, Mary Hyland and Lily Kempson, were not afraid to use force to achieve their objectives. Indeed Hyland apparently used a bayonet to oblige a milkman to hand over some of his wares and Kempson held up a bread delivery man at gunpoint.[67]

When Nurse Elizabeth O'Farrell delivered Pearse's order to stand down, Mallin and Markievicz surrendered to Captain Harry de Courcy-Wheeler, a barrister by profession, who was serving as staff officer to General Lowe. The surrender was made rather awkward by the fact that Markievicz was a first cousin of de Courcy-Wheeler's wife. Markievicz kissed her small revolver reverently before handing it over.

Constance Markievicz in her ICA uniform, probably taken in Dublin *c*. 1915–16.

Commandant Mallin and Constance
Markievicz, the leaders of the Stephen's
Green garrison, under arrest.

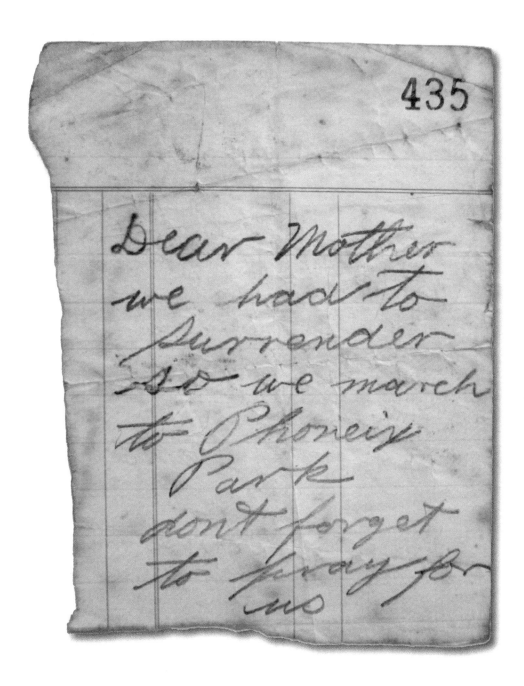

This note, which reads 'Dear Mother, we had to surrender so we march to Phoenix Park, don't forget to pray for us', was given to Fr Aloysius by Matthew Hand of 12 Great Longford Street, Dublin, who served with the ICA under Michael Mallin. He was subsequently dispatched to the detention camp at Frongoch.

The Royal College of Surgeons.

Opposite: The front cover of *Le Miroir*, the illustrated French newspaper, dated 21 May 1916, showing Constance Markievicz in a British ambulance en route to prison after her sentencing.

Sixième année. — N° 130.   Le Numéro : **25** centimes.   DIMANCHE 21 Mai 1916.

LE MIROIR

PUBLICATION HEBDOMADAIRE, 18, Rue d'Enghien, PARIS

*LE MIROIR paie n'importe quel prix les documents photographiques relatifs à la guerre,
présentant un intérêt particulier.*

LA COMTESSE MARKIEVICZ REGAGNE LA PRISON APRÈS SA CONDAMNATION

La comtesse Constance Markievicz est vue ici avec la nurse chargée de la surveiller dans l'auto qui la ramena
en prison en sortant de la cour martiale. Sa peine de mort a été commuée en travaux forcés à perpétuité.

Rosie Hackett

Among the most remarkable women present in the Royal College of Surgeons during the week of the Easter Rising was Rosie Hackett, a woman of such unbending resolve that Dublin City Council chose to name a new city bridge in her honour in 2013. Born in 1893, she grew up in the tenements around Eden Quay where she initially worked as a packer in a paper store.

In 1911 Hackett was among the women who went on strike at the Jacob's biscuit factory. A co-founder of the IWWU, she was in the crowd baton-charged by the Dublin Metropolitan Police on 'Bloody Sunday' 1913. During the Lockout, she was one of the stalwarts of the Liberty Hall soup kitchens and became a close confidante of James Connolly. When the strike finished, Hackett helped to run the co-op shop at Liberty Hall, as well as organising cultural events to entertain ITGWU members.

The Rising came as no surprise to Hackett. She was on first-name terms with those who planned it. Whenever they came to Liberty Hall, she greeted them and escorted them up to Connolly. She studied first aid with Dr Kathleen Lynn for six months before the Rising. She also took part in numerous night marches with the ICA.

In the weeks before the Rising, Hackett was kept busy putting together first-aid kits and knapsacks. By Holy Thursday she was slicing ham and shaping sandwiches. On the night of Easter Sunday she was flat out 'going back and forth with messages'.[68] As she later explained, 'I was small, and would get to places, unnoticed; and I was always successful.'[69] It is said, but sadly unproven, that she carried the original Proclamation from the printing press up to Connolly, the paper still damp with ink.

The following morning, Easter Monday, she was sent as a nurse to St Stephen's Green under Michael Mallin and Constance Markievicz. Before she left, Dr Lynn gave her a white coat that went down to her toes. 'I remember Plunkett and some other men were laughing at the coat touching the ground,' wrote Hackett.[70]

On Easter Tuesday, after a brief sleep on a mattress at the Royal College of Surgeons, Hackett got up for a cup of tea. A man named Murray lay down in her place only to be shot in the face moments later – he died in St Vincent's Hospital later that week.

Hackett vividly recalled the despair when they received Pearse's command to surrender. Markievicz crumpled on a stairwell, her head in her hands. Mallin, 'terribly pale' and haggard, 'shaking hands with all of us'.[71] Hackett was arrested and imprisoned in Kilmainham Gaol for ten days. After her release, she teamed up with the Irish suffragettes Louie Bennett and Helen Chenevix to reorganise the IWWU, in which she remained active for the rest of her life.

On the first anniversary of the Rising, Hackett displayed her customary gusto when she teamed up with Helena Molony, Jinny Shanahan and Brigid Davis to hang a banner from Liberty Hall inscribed 'James Connolly Murdered May 12th 1916'. The authorities in Dublin Castle panicked and sent a force of 400 policemen to take it down. 'I always felt that it was worth it,' wrote Hackett, 'to see all the trouble the police had in getting it down. No one was arrested. Of course, if it took 400 policemen to take four women – what would the newspapers say?'[72]

Hackett ran the ITGWU tobacco and sweet shop at Eden Quay until its closure in 1957. One of the happiest moments of her life came in 1970 when she was awarded the gold medal for devoting sixty years of her life to the trade-union movement. She lived with her bachelor brother, Tommy, in Fairview until her death in 1976 at the age of eighty-four. She was buried in Glasnevin Cemetery with full military honours.

Liberty Hall with the banner 'James Connolly Murdered May 12th 1916' hung on the outside.

ATTENDING TO THE WOUNDED

Photo by] [Stanley.
Dr. ELLA WEBB, Lady District Superintendent St.
John Ambulance Brigade, Dublin.

While the fighting raged around the city, the growing number of casualties, civilian and combatant alike, needed urgent medical aid. Many of the wounded, particularly civilians, still lay where they had fallen. Anyone who wanted to help risked being caught in the crossfire themselves, be they ambulance personnel endeavouring to tend to them on the street, or doctors and nurses trying to reach the hospitals in order to treat the wounded.

One group in particular that distinguished itself with its excellent service to the wounded during the Rising was the St John Ambulance Brigade under the leadership of Dr John Lumsden. One of Dr Lumsden's deputies was Dr Ella Webb, a former student of Alexandra College, Dublin, and medical officer to St Patrick's Dispensary for Women and Children.[73] Dr Webb was responsible for converting the Irish War Hospital Supply Depot at 14 Merrion Square into an improvised emergency hospital during the Rising. She went from house to house 'begging and borrowing items of linen and other necessities'.[74] She also cycled daily through the firing line to visit the hospital, where the Brigade treated casualties on both sides, as well as feeding and tending to evacuees. When one St John's ambulance brought nine casualties from the Adelaide Hospital to the emergency hospital on Merrion Square, Dr Lumsden sent the ambulance back laden with fresh provisions as the Adelaide was completely cut off from supplies.

Founded in 1887, the Brigade was a subsidiary of the St John Ambulance Association, a foundation of the Order of St John, and comprised uniformed volunteers who were on standby to render first aid to the sick and injured. The Dublin (St James' Gate) Ambulance Division was formed in 1903 at the Guinness Brewery at St James's Gate. It was placed under the guidance of Dr Lumsden, medical officer for Guinness, who was well known for the excellence of the first-aid classes he gave to the brewery's employees. From 1905 the public were invited to join a second unit, the City of Dublin Ambulance Division. Women were finally allowed to join when the first nursing division was formed in 1909.

The Brigade was closely involved during the Lockout, looking after casualties from clashes such as the Sackville Street baton charge. With the outbreak of war in Europe, many Brigade members served as part of the Voluntary Aid Detachment, providing auxiliary medical aid for those injured in combat.

During the Rising the Brigade was active in the St Stephen's Green area, as well as at Jacob's biscuit factory, Charlemont Street and Clanwilliam House.[75] On Easter Wednesday intense fighting broke out around the City of Dublin Hospital on Baggot Street and ambulance drivers were warned not to go into the area. However, Lumsden refused to leave the wounded unattended and advanced into the danger zone alone, where he spent several hours tending to their injuries.[76]

Another member of the Brigade who served during the Rising was John Francis Homan, the first principal of the Wharf Boys' School in East Wall, whose colourful life story includes an unauthorised leave of absence to visit Japan during its war with Russia.

Dr Ella Webb was awarded an MBE and appointed anaesthetist to the Adelaide Hospital in 1918, thereby becoming the first woman member of the Adelaide's medical staff. Homan became a prominent member of Cumann na nGaedheal in north Dublin and continued on as principal of the Wharf Boys' School until his retirement in 1926. Lumsden was knighted by George V and he remained Commissioner of the Brigade until his death in 1944.

CITY HALL AND DUBLIN CASTLE

On Easter Monday most of the Dublin Castle garrison had gone to the Fairyhouse races to watch the Irish Grand National – this was one of the key factors taken into account when the leaders rescheduled the rebellion for that day. Soon after the soldiers departed, a company of the ICA comprising sixteen men and nine women under the command of the Abbey actor Seán Connolly made for City Hall on Dublin's Dame Street. Their orders were to prevent the race-going British soldiers from returning to the nearby Castle and gaining access to their weapons and ammunition.

Shortly before midday, Constable James O'Brien, from Kilfergus near Glin, Co. Limerick, was on guard at the Cork Hill entrance to Dublin Castle when a Volunteer from Connolly's company cycled up to the entrance. Realising something was awry, the unarmed forty-eight-year-old O'Brien was attempting to close the gate when the Volunteer shot him dead.[77]

According to some accounts, it was Connolly who killed Constable O'Brien, while others claim Connolly was so appalled by the murder that he made a snap decision to rush the Castle gate directly. Six men charged into the castle guardhouse where they overpowered three soldiers and bound them with their own puttees. Uncertain about the strength of the British military within the Castle, Connolly left the six men at the guardhouse and headed for City Hall. Had he known how limited the British resources actually were, Connolly's company could probably have captured Dublin Castle at that point. Instead, the Castle complex was to serve as the headquarters of British operations for the remainder of the Rising.[78]

Seán Connolly, commander of the City Hall garrison, who was killed on Easter Monday.

After failing to take the Castle, the Volunteers took possession of both City Hall and the offices of the Dublin *Daily Express*. Members of the garrison were posted on the roof of City Hall to command the approaches to the Castle from Dame Street, Castle Street, and from Cork Hill to the Upper Castle Yard. Shortly after two o'clock Seán Connolly was shot dead on the roof by a sniper operating from the Castle clock tower, while attempting to hoist a green flag to the top of the City Hall dome. Dr Kathleen Lynn, who was with the Volunteers there, noted that there was nothing she could do to save him and that he died almost immediately. Helena Molony prayed over him as he lay dying.

A couple of hours after the shooting at the Castle gate, a troop of perhaps 180 British soldiers poured out of the nearby Ship Street Barracks and began firing at City Hall. Two ICA women, Molly O'Reilly and, later, Helena Molony, were sent to the GPO to ask for reinforcements. That evening James Connolly sent just eight men, led by George Norgrove. On Monday night the British launched a full-scale offensive on the position and by early Tuesday morning it was clear to the garrison that they could not hold the position against such superior forces and they surrendered. As well as Seán Connolly, the ICA based in City Hall and the surrounding area lost three men and an ICA boy scout, Charles Darcy, who was just fifteen years old.[79]

Constable James O'Brien, pictured here in the uniform of the Dublin Metropolitan Police.

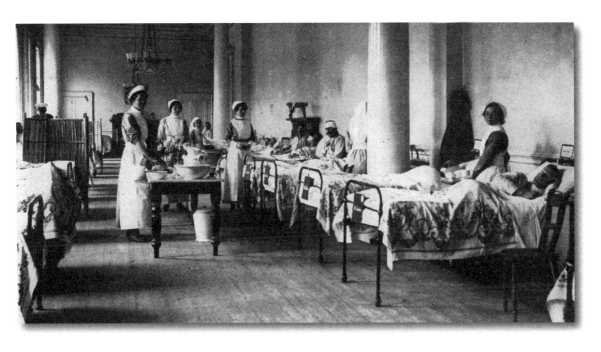

Above: British soldiers wounded during the Rising recuperate in a makeshift hospital ward at Dublin Castle.

Left: This is a scene from a play called *The Memory of the Dead*, written and directed by Casimir Dunin Markievicz and staged at both the Abbey and the Gaiety theatres in Dublin by his Independent Dramatic Company in 1910. The play was probably co-written by his wife, Constance, who starred in the production along with Seán (or Seaghan as he is named on the bill) Connolly (*in the chair*), George Nesbitt (*lying on the floor*), Mervyn Columb (*officer standing*), Edward Keegan and a young Patrick McCartan (*kneeling*). Set against the backdrop of the 1798 Rising, it concerns a rebel leader who is saved by a patriot girl called Norah Doyle. The play later toured Ireland and it is said that Helena Molony took on the role of Norah, while Connolly was the rebel leader.

Kathleen Lynn

Born in Co. Mayo, Kathleen Lynn was the daughter of a Church of Ireland clergyman. Devoting herself to medical studies, she was only the third woman to be awarded a Fellowship of the Royal College of Surgeons in Ireland. Dr Lynn became a suffragette and joined the ICA. She served as Chief Medical Officer of the rebel forces during the Rising. She also took command of the City Hall garrison following Seán Connolly's death and, as such, it was she who tendered the garrison's surrender in the early hours of Tuesday morning, following a successful British assault on their position. When asked about her role, she defiantly stated that she was 'a Red Cross doctor and a belligerent'.[80]

Lynn was imprisoned in Ship Street Barracks for a week, where she instigated a de-lousing campaign. After a brief spell in Kilmainham Gaol, she was deported to England where Jennie Wyse Power secured her a job with a doctor near Bath. She returned to Ireland in the autumn of 1916.

In 1919 Lynn and her companion Madeleine Ffrench-Mullen established St Ultan's Hospital for Infants to treat and support infants and mothers and to reduce infant mortality – child-mortality rates in Ireland were the highest in Europe at the time. The hospital included one of the first 'Montessori wards' in the world.

As well as her medical achievements, Lynn remained a committed republican. In 1917 she became a member of the Sinn Féin executive and was forced to go on the run when the British authorities began arresting people due to the so-called 'German Plot', an alleged conspiracy between republicans and Germany to start another insurrection. When Dáil Éireann was established in 1919 she was appointed Director of Public Health. During the

Civil War she aided anti-Treaty republicans and both her house and St Ultan's were frequently raided.

When Dr Lynn died in 1955, she was buried with full military honours.

Dr Kathleen Lynn holding four babies shortly after St Ultan's opened its doors to the public.

'Who fears to speak of Easter Week?' A rare republican poster published by the Devin-Adair Publishing Company of New York in 1916, comprising a ballad sheet and lyrics surrounded by portrait vignettes of the Rising's patriots. Founded in New York by Henry Garrity in 1911, Devin-Adair was well known at the time for its publication of Irish poetry and books on popular ornithology.

THE PACIFIST AND THE SOLDIER

Born in Bailieborough, Co. Cavan, in 1878, Francis Sheehy-Skeffington attended UCD, where his highbrow circle of friends included James Joyce and Tom Kettle. Always unconventional, his university attire consisted of knickerbockers, long socks and a badge that read 'Votes for Women'. Joyce nicknamed him 'Hairy Jesus' on account of his ethical ideals.[81] A supporter of Home Rule, he did not agree with the Irish Volunteers because an armed militia ran contrary to his pacifism. On the other hand, his wife, Hanna, who had co-founded the Irish Women's Franchise League in 1908, spent the duration of the Rising dispatching food supplies to the rebels located in both the GPO and the Royal College of Surgeons.

On Easter Monday Sheehy-Skeffington chanced to be on Dame Street when the City Hall garrison opened fire on Dublin Castle. Having watched a young British officer fall to the ground, he and a chemist who was based nearby ran through a hail of gunfire towards the Castle, armed with bandages. However, as they came in sight of the gate, they saw the officer's body being hauled back into the courtyard by two of his fellow soldiers. Later that night Hanna berated her husband for running such a risk. 'I could not let anyone bleed to death while I could help,' he replied.[82]

The man whom Sheehy-Skeffington tried to save was Guy Vickery Pinfield, a twenty-one-year-old cavalry officer with the 8th King's Royal Irish Hussars. Born in Bishop's Stortford, Hertfordshire, in 1895, Pinfield's grandfather was a Liverpool dock solicitor who rose to become a major tea planter in the Indian province of Assam. The family was closely connected to the department-store tycoon Sir John Barker, and to Sir Walter Gilbey, the British wine merchant and sometime president of the Royal Agricultural Society. Pinfield's first cousin Anthony Simkins would serve as Deputy Director of MI5 from 1965 until his retirement in 1971.

Educated at Marlborough College and Clare College, Cambridge, Pinfield played rugby for Rosslyn Park Rugby Football Club in south-west London. When the First World War began, he secured a commission with the Hussars. In 1915 he was posted to Ireland to train with the 10th Reserve Cavalry Regiment at the Curragh Camp in Co. Kildare.

On the afternoon of Easter Monday, Pinfield was shot by a volley of sniper fire while he and a group of Hussars tried to enter Dublin Castle. Despite the best efforts of his colleagues, he did not survive, thus becoming the first British officer to die in the Rising.

His body was wrapped in a winding sheet and buried in a temporary grave in the Castle gardens. Many of the British soldiers killed that week were buried beside him. In May 1916 the families of the British fallen came to the Castle to reclaim the bodies. At the end of the month, the unclaimed were given military funerals and reinterred in the British military cemetery at Blackhorse Avenue, Grangegorman. However, Pinfield and four other officers remained at the Castle, buried in what was then a formal garden attached to the state apartments. Perhaps Guy Pinfield's family felt it was a fitting burial place at the time, but by the time these 'temporary' graves were rediscovered in 1962, the garden was utterly overgrown. The Imperial War Graves Commission made arrangements for the five bodies to be exhumed, and they were reinterred in Grangegorman in 1963.

In 2011 there was renewed interest in the story of Guy Pinfield when a mystery Irish buyer paid £850 (€1,000) at an auction in south-east England for a five-carat gold memorial locket containing his portrait, which his desolate mother had worn after his death. Engraved with the Hussar's motto *Pristinae virtutis memores* (the memory of former valour), it also has Pinfield's initials 'GVP' and his place and date of death, 'Dublin April 24th

1916'. The identity of the buyer may remain a mystery, but Pinfield is clearly not forgotten. His fellow officers erected a brass plate to his memory in St Patrick's Cathedral, Dublin. His name was also etched in marble on monuments at Marlborough College, his rugby club in Rosslyn Park and at both the church and war memorial in Bishop's Stortford.

It is unlikely that Sheehy-Skeffington ever learned what became of the man he tried to help. The day after Pinfield died, the venerable pacifist returned to the streets in an attempt to discourage a growing mob of looters. He was arrested in Rathmines, south Dublin, and, along with two journalists, Thomas Dickson and Patrick MacIntyre, he was taken to Portobello Barracks. Dickson and MacIntyre were both loyalists who had openly expressed their opposition to the Rising. Despite this, all three men were summarily executed by firing squad the following day on the orders of a British officer called Captain John C. Bowen-Colthurst, who was suffering from severe shell shock following his experiences on the Western Front.

After the Rising, Bowen-Colthurst was tried for these deaths and for the killing of two other men, nineteen-year-old James Joseph Coade and Volunteer Richard O'Carroll, both of whom he shot himself. Found guilty but insane, he served just eighteen months in the Broadmoor Criminal Lunatic Asylum. He then emigrated to Montreal, Canada, where he died aged eighty-five in 1965.

Sean O'Casey would later write, 'In Sheehy-Skeffington, and not in [James] Connolly, fell the first martyr to Irish Socialism, for he linked Ireland not only with the little nations struggling for self-expression, but with the world's Humanity struggling for a higher life.'[83]

BOLAND'S MILL

EDWARD DE VALERA
President of the IRISH Republic. 1919

Éamon de Valera.

When Éamon de Valera completed his second term as president of Ireland in 1973, one of his first stops was at Boland's Bakery, now the Treasury Building, at the southern entrance to the Grand Canal Docks. This was where the wily Irish statesman had gained his first real revolutionary experience fifty-seven years earlier, when, as a young mathematician, he served as commandant of the 3rd Battalion and adjutant of the Dublin Brigade during the Rising.

Shortly after noon on Easter Monday de Valera and approximately 100 members of the 3rd Battalion stormed the premises of Boland's Bakery and told all the bakers working there to go home. Both the mill and bakery had been identified as vital strategic locations, and control of them would enable the rebels to prevent British reinforcements crossing the two bridges over the docks, as well as the bridge by Lower Mount Street. They would also provide a key vantage point over the railway lines running between Sandymount and Westland Row, and the main road between the port at Kingstown (Dún Laoghaire) and the city centre.

Having secured control of Boland's, de Valera established an outpost in Westland Row (now Pearse) Railway Station where the men quickly ripped out the railway tracks on the Kingstown line to prevent troop trains getting too close. De Valera established his own headquarters in the dispensary beside the bakery. He ordered the removal of essential parts from the gasworks and the electricity supply station in Ringsend, thus cutting off the gas supply and immobilising the electric trams.

Some men were sent to Mount Street Bridge and others to cover the entrance to the British military barracks at Beggar's Bush. Due to a lack of manpower, de Valera was unable to organise scouting parties, and he was thus unaware that the barracks was in fact virtually empty.

On the Thursday of Easter Week the gunboat *Helga* began shelling de Valera's base at Boland's. A second naval gun was taken ashore from *Helga* and set up in Percy Place. De Valera deftly neutralised the danger by flying a rebel flag from a nearby distillery, which attracted much of the subsequent shelling. The Boland's garrison remained on alert for the rest of the week, anticipating a major assault by the British forces, but it just didn't happen. One night de Valera and some men slipped out to a nearby railway embankment where they silently watched the city burning to the west.

The garrison held out until Sunday when Nurse Elizabeth O'Farrell delivered Pearse's order to surrender to de Valera. At first he thought that this was a British ploy, but when he was finally convinced that it was genuine, he instructed his men to ensure all arms were put out of action lest they be of use to the enemy. None of his men were prepared to carry the white flag of surrender, so it fell to a Red Cross worker to hold it while de Valera's vice-commandant, Joseph O'Connor, marched the men out onto Grattan Street where they were ordered to 'ground arms'. It galled de Valera to see the local people coming out from their homes to offer cups of tea to the British soldiers while ridiculing the Volunteers for their actions. 'If only you had come out to help us,' he chided, 'even with knives, you would not behold us like this.'[84]

After their surrender, de Valera and his men were held for two nights in bull stalls at the Royal Dublin Society's (RDS) Showgrounds in Ballsbridge.[85] On Tuesday morning they were transferred to Richmond Barracks, where there was already a queue of prisoners waiting to be tried.

The delay was to save de Valera's life. When he finally stood for his trial by court martial on 8 May he was, like all battalion commandants, sentenced to death. However, the executions of the main ringleaders earlier in the week had already generated such a negative effect on public opinion that his death sentence was commuted to penal servitude for life. His US citizenship was not used in his favour and he himself made no claims on that basis.

de Valera with members of the Sherwood Foresters at Richmond Barracks.

THE BATTLE OF MOUNT STREET BRIDGE

By lunchtime on Wednesday 26 April some 12,000 British troops had arrived in Dublin. Among them were 2,000 untested officers and soldiers from the Sherwood Foresters who came marching up Northumberland Road from Kingstown, en route to oust the rebel leaders from the GPO.

One of the officers was a barrister from Nottingham called Frederick Christian Dietrichsen, who had married a Mitchell from the Dublin family of wine merchants. Dietrichsen's two small daughters had been sent to Dublin for safety following growing fears of German zeppelin raids in England. They were in Blackrock, waving flags on the pavement, when the Foresters marched through. When Dietrichsen saw them, he dropped out of the column and flung his arms around the children before resuming his place with his men.[86]

The Foresters then paused at the RDS's premises in Ballsbridge, where Lord Rathdonnell, president of the RDS, was attempting to host the Spring Show, a major annual cattle and livestock exhibition. John Evelyn Wrench, one of Rathdonnell's colleagues, recalled meeting the troopers on that 'very hot day'. The Foresters he talked with were primarily miners, farmers and factory workers who had signed up to fight Germans, little imagining they would be posted to tackle a rebellion in Ireland. 'One British regiment consisted of young recruits, such a nice lot of boys,' wrote Wrench. 'We brought them lemonade, for which they were most grateful.'[87]

As the Foresters approached Mount Street Bridge, they were in for a big surprise. De Valera had surveyed the area carefully in the preceding weeks. He had considered the military possibilities, and his planning was about

Lord Rathdonnell, president of the RDS, was attempting to hold the Spring Show in Ballsbridge during the week of the Rising. Shortly before the Sherwood Foresters advanced to Mount Street Bridge, they paused at the RDS for lemonade.

Michael Malone, a carpenter by trade, was shot dead in the battle with the Foresters. Malone's brother Willie was in the Irish Volunteers, but, answering Red-mond's call, he joined the Royal Dublin Fusiliers, only to be killed in Flanders.

to pay off. On his command, a unit of Volunteers, led by Mick Malone, made its way into this leafy and strongly unionist part of the city and occupied Clanwilliam House, Carisbrooke House, the local parochial hall and schoolhouse, and 25 Northumberland Road. These buildings enjoyed commanding views over the bridge across the Grand Canal, ensuring the Volunteers were perfectly positioned to orchestrate a devastating crossfire ambush.

The first phase of the battle of Mount Street Bridge had occurred two days earlier, during the afternoon of Easter Monday. The Georgius Rex defence force was made up of older men, many of whom were veterans of the Anglo-Boer War. They had been deemed too old to serve on the front line and formed a sort of home guard. The 'Gorgeous Wrecks', as they were dubbed, had been on manoeuvre in Kingstown and were returning to barracks when they learned of the Rising. They carried weapons but no ammunition. As they approached the city they split into two sections. One, led by Major Harris of the Trinity OTC, came under fire from Boland's. The other, led by Frank 'Chicken' Browning, the Chairman of the Irish Rugby Football Union and a first-class cricketer, marched along Northumberland Road. Malone's men opened fire and four of the veterans, including Browning, fell dead before the Volunteers realised they had no ammunition and ceased fire. The remainder of the Georgius Rex then rapidly withdrew to Beggar's Bush.

Like the men of Georgius Rex, the Foresters walked into a death trap. Twelve fell in the opening volley, and there was little let-up in a battle that ultimately lasted from noon to 8 p.m., save for a brief ceasefire while nurses and doctors from nearby Sir Patrick Dun's Hospital attended to and removed some of the wounded. They were assisted by three clergymen, Fr McNevin, Fr McCann and the Rev. Mr Hall of Dalkey. Four British officers and 216 soldiers were killed or maimed that day, marking almost half the total British military losses for the whole week of the Rising. Captain F. C. Dietrichsen was among the first to die.

Frank Browning. Following his death in the Rising he was buried in Deansgrange Cemetery, Co. Dublin, beneath a headstone that honours 'an honourable comrade and true and distinguished sportsman'. He was survived by his young widow and their small son.

Below: The survivors of the Mount Street Bridge garrison of the Dublin Brigade who took on the Sherwood Foresters and inflicted some of the heaviest British casualties of the Rising. *Standing* (left to right): Thomas (or James) Walsh, Patrick Doyle, Paddy Roe, James (or Thomas) Walsh. *Seated*: Daniel Byrne, Seamus 'Jimmy' Grace, Joe Clarke. *Sitting on ground*: William Ronan and James Doyle.

The Foresters' stubborn and successive attempts to charge the Volunteers' positions were utterly suicidal, not least when they could simply have made their way up to Baggot Street Bridge instead. Nor did it help the British cause when they were misinformed that the invisible snipers were based in St Stephen's Schoolhouse on Northumberland Road, which had in fact been vacated by its defenders. 'It always seemed to me such a wanton waste of life,' remarked J. E. Wrench, 'though we tried to explain to them as well as we could the geography of the streets in that part of Dublin and what they might expect.'[88]

It was not until a second battalion of Foresters arrived on Wednesday afternoon with heavy artillery and began shelling the sniper posts that the British forces gained the upper hand. They also moved into Percy Place, a vital escape route for the Volunteers, and showered the premises at 25 Northumberland Road with grenades. Northumberland Road, which had been manned by just two men, Lieutenant Mick Malone and Jimmy Grace, was the first position to fall, soon followed by the parochial hall. Malone was killed in the battle. Grace had an incredibly lucky escape, successfully hiding behind a stove in the basement when the British seized the building.[89]

Led by Section Commander George Reynolds, the men at Clanwilliam House held out the longest; the post finally fell on Wednesday evening when the building was engulfed by fire. Reynolds died alongside Section Commander Patrick Doyle and Richard Murphy. Their bodies were consumed in the flames.

A memorial to the four slain Volunteers stands by Mount Street Bridge today. There is no such remembrance for the Foresters who perished, many of whom were buried in the military cemetery at Grangegorman. Nor is there a memorial to Holden Stodart of the St John Ambulance Brigade, who was killed in the crossfire while tending to the wounded.[90]

The ruins of 25 Northumberland Road, where Section Commander Seamus 'Jimmy' Grace and Lieutenant Michael 'Mick' Malone took up position.

The ruins of Clanwilliam House after the battle of Mount Street Bridge. The three-storey Georgian building, which commanded an excellent view of both the canal bridge and Northumberland Road, was occupied by Section Commander George Reynolds, Daniel Byrne, William Ronan and James Doyle, while Richard Murphy, Patrick Doyle, Thomas Walsh and James Walsh later reinforced the position.

Members of the Sherwood Foresters taking a breather on Northumberland Road after the battle.

Left to right: Section Commander George Reynolds, Patrick Doyle and Richard Murphy. The three men were killed at Clanwilliam House during the battle of Mount Street Bridge. Raised in Ringsend, Reynolds was a long-term Gaelic Leaguer who worked as an ecclesiastical artist.

THE END COMES

By the morning of Friday 28 April, incendiary devices were raining down on the GPO and had set the upper stories of the building alight, along with much of Sackville Street. At dusk that day the members of the Provisional Government realised that their position was no longer tenable and Patrick Pearse informed the garrison that they would have to evacuate. The plan was to take up a new position in Great Britain (now Parnell) Street, at the William and Woods' factory. At 8 p.m. an advance party led by The O'Rahilly left by a side entrance in an attempt to clear the way up Moore Street. They failed in their mission but, as flames began to engulf the GPO, the men inside were compelled to take their chances.

The prisoners who had been held in the GPO since Easter Monday were released and the garrison then exited in small groups. Pearse and James Connolly were among the last to leave, with the latter, now unable to walk due to his injuries, being carried out on a stretcher. The men took refuge in houses on both sides of Moore Street. They then began to bore their way through the internal walls of the houses which enabled them to proceed up the street unexposed to British fire. However, with Dublin burning all around him and civilian and Volunteer casualties continuing to mount, Pearse decided that it was time to surrender. He may have felt compelled to act after witnessing three unarmed, elderly men on Moore Street being scythed down by a machine gun despite the fact they were waving a white flag.

All the remaining leaders agreed with Pearse's decision except for Tom Clarke, who wanted to fight on. Nurse Elizabeth O'Farrell, wearing a Red Cross insignia and carrying a white flag, was then sent to deliver the message of surrender to Brigadier General Lowe. O'Farrell, a member of Cumann na mBan, had been in the GPO throughout the fighting and earned immense respect for her bravery acting as a go-between for Pearse and the British authorities.

Walter Stanley Paget's depiction of 'Scene in the GPO, Dublin, just before its evacuation' evokes a situation in which James Connolly lies severely wounded, with his secretary Winnie Carney offering him a drink. Tom Clarke looks straight at the beholder while Joe Plunkett is depicted with his arms crossed, sporting an Irish Volunteers slouch hat and a scarf. The London-born Walter Paget, a friend of Jack B. Yeats, was immortalised by his illustrator brother, Sidney, who used him as a model for his drawings of Sherlock Holmes in the original Arthur Conan Doyle books.

At 2.30 p.m. on Saturday 29 April, Pearse surrendered his sword to Brigadier General Lowe, second-in-command to General Maxwell, on Great Britain Street at the top of Moore Street. The remaining men of the GPO garrison were allowed to march into captivity with their weapons, while the women of Moore Street pelted them with rotten vegetables and the contents of their chamber pots.[91] All that was left to do was to let the other remaining garrisons know of the surrender, and Elizabeth O'Farrell was once again drafted in to help.

By Sunday the Rising was over.

The surrender of Patrick Pearse to Brigadier General Lowe. Nurse Elizabeth O'Farrell, who arranged the meeting between Pearse and Lowe, is just hidden from view behind Pearse. She remained an active republican until her death in 1957. Lowe's son John on the near left went on to become Hollywood actor John Loder (see page 248).

Michael Rahilly (The O'Rahilly)

Born in Ballylongford on the most westerly banks of the river Shannon in 1875, Michael Rahilly's family connection to the small north Kerry town ran back to at least 1809, when his great-grandfather, also called Michael, built a two-storey pub there. By 1861 The O'Rahilly's entrepreneurial father, Richard, had expanded the business to such an extent that he was variously described as baker, draper, grocer, fish-curer, miller, farmer, landowner, importer, inventor, postmaster, shipping agent, general merchant and, perhaps most importantly, publican. If you go to the pub today, you can still see the yardstick used by the in-house tailors to measure arm lengths. Customers would sit at the bar and drink a pint or two, while their tailor proposed different colours and cloths.

Richard was undoubtedly the wealthiest man in the area. He is even said to have had the first refrigerator in Ireland. When he died from pneumonia in 1896, he left his estate to his wife, Ellen, and his business to his son, Michael. However, where Richard was a prudent investor, loyal to the crown, Michael was a deeply compulsive man whose opinions were increasingly at odds with the British Establishment in Ireland.

In 1898 Michael sold his father's businesses in Ballylongford and sailed for New York with an engagement ring in his pocket. In April the following year he married his 'darling Nancy'. Nancy Browne was the daughter of a Philadelphia businessman, and from 1905 to 1908 the couple lived in Philadelphia's fashionable Drexel Hill suburb.

When the Rahillys returned from the USA, Michael became involved in the Sinn Féin movement. He also became interested in the history of old Irish clans and, in reaction to the British crown's practice of awarding titles to 'loyal' Irish subjects, he took the name 'The O'Rahilly'.[92]

In 1913 he became a co-founder and treasurer of the Irish Volunteers. In April 1914 he was on the pier in Howth to greet Erskine Childers when the yacht *Asgard* sailed in with a cargo of German guns for the Irish Volunteers. Although strongly opposed to the Rising and livid about the abduction of Bulmer Hobson, he arrived at Liberty Hall in his motorcar on Easter Monday, approaching Pearse and Connolly with the fine words, 'I helped wind this clock and I've come to hear it strike.'[93]

He remained in the GPO until the Friday when, with the building on fire, he led a party out to find an escape route up Moore Street. As the Volunteers made their way towards Great Britain (now Parnell) Street they were confronted by a barricade, constructed across the top of the street by Sergeant Major Samuel Lomas and a dozen fellow British soldiers. To create an effective blockade, the soldiers had raided the nearby butcher's shop of Messrs Simpson and Wallace, taking the butcher's block, as well as bedding, bedsteads, wardrobes, mattresses and an armchair in which Lomas managed to get some shut-eye. An alert British machine-gunner from Lomas' company spotted The O'Rahilly and his men and opened fire. The O'Rahilly and some of those with him were hit. The Kerryman managed to crawl into a doorway at the corner of Moore Street and Sackville Lane, where he wrote a poignant letter to Nancy, sending 'tons & tons of love dearie to you & the boys & to Nell & Anna'. 'It was a good fight anyhow,' he concluded. 'Goodbye Darling.'[94] He died there some hours later.

He was immortalised in a 1938 poem by W. B. Yeats called 'The O'Rahilly':

> Sing of the O'Rahilly,
> Do not deny his right;
> Sing a 'the' before his name;
> Allow that he, despite
> All those learned historians,
> Established it for good;
> He wrote out that word himself,
> He christened himself with blood.
> *How goes the weather?*

The O'Rahilly was the most senior member of the Irish Volunteers to die in action. As he awaited his execution the following week, Patrick Pearse reputedly said, 'I envy O'Rahilly – that is the way I wanted to die.'[95]

Company Sergeant Major Samuel H. Lomas of the Sherwood Foresters won a Distinguished Conduct Medal for his courage at Moore Street where he led his men on a series of missions to storm enemy posts along the street. He later served as the senior NCO at the executions of Pearse, MacDonagh and Clarke. Lomas was killed on active service in France on 27 April 1917; his body was never recovered and he is commemorated on the Thiepval Memorial to the Missing at the Somme. His diary from the Rising was published in *The 1916 Diaries of an Irish Rebel and a British Soldier* by Mick O'Farrell in 2014.

The doorway of Leahy Brothers public house at the corner of Moore Street and Sackville Lane (now O'Rahilly Parade) where The O'Rahilly died. His last words to his 'dearest Nancy' are now engraved on the wall beside it.

Nicknamed 'The O'Tatur', T. W. Murphy, the sub-editor of *The Motor News*, went out with his camera soon after the Rising. He is pictured here standing beside the burned-out shell of The O'Rahilly's car on Prince's Street to the side of the GPO.

A makeshift barricade at Prince's Street to the side of the GPO comprising the remains of a taxi (*left*) and The O'Rahilly's De Dion-Bouton (*right*).

John Loder/Lowe

One of the more unusual men to serve in the British Army during the Rising was the future Hollywood actor John Loder. Born in 1898, he was christened William John Muir Lowe, and was a son of Brigadier General William Lowe to whom Pearse surrendered at the close of the Rising. Indeed, he served as his father's aide-de-camp during the Rising and so he was afforded an unusual perspective. After the surrender, he was instructed to escort Pearse to Kilmainham Gaol. In his memoirs he recalled how Pearse gave his gold watch, chain and ring to a priest travelling with them, presumably to hold for his mother or sister. 'When we reached the jail gates he had not finished giving his last messages to his family, so I told the driver to keep on driving. When Pearse had finished, he turned to me and said, "That was kind of you. I would like to give you a small token of my gratitude." He took off his hat, removed the Sinn Féin badge and handed it to me.'[96]

Lowe (or Loder) went on to fight at the Somme and was captured by the Germans, but he survived the First World War and made his way to Hollywood, USA, where he caught the eye of the director Alexander Korda. Cecil B. DeMille later cast him in *The Doctor's Secret*, Paramount's first talking picture, a seminal moment in the history of cinema. He also played a wealthy widower engaged to Bette Davis in the 1942 drama *Now Voyager*.

A member of the Loyal Dublin Volunteers, a Dublin-based unionist paramilitary force, on guard duty at the GPO after the Rising.

Soldiers and reservists on the march outside the GPO. The three men in the foreground are regular soldiers while the two on the outer edges are from the Irish Association of Volunteer Training Corps (VTC) armed with RIC carbines. The association comprised a number of different civilian units such as the Veterans Corps, the Dublin Motor Cyclists Corps and the Irish Rugby Football Union Corps. Frank Browning, the president of the latter, was killed in the Rising at an ambush near Beggar's Bush Barracks. T. W. Murphy, who took the photograph, was the organiser and honorary secretary of the Dublin Motor Cyclists' VTC. Although non-political, some VTC members previously belonged to the Loyal Dublin Volunteers. The man on the far left appears to have a Dublin Metropolitan Police duty band on his sleeve.

Above: A rare smile from women and children returning home with fresh firewood scavenged from the debris of the Rising.

Overleaf: Irish prisoners being marched along Bachelor's Walk under the guard of the British military.

INSURRECTION ACROSS
IRELAND

ENNISCORTHY, CO. WEXFORD

One of the few places outside Dublin where the Volunteers made a major impact during the Rising was Enniscorthy, a town with a proud history of rebellion and strong support for the IRB. The Enniscorthy Volunteers were initially commanded by W. J. Brennan-Whitmore, who fought in Dublin during the Rising, but he had resigned amid an internal quarrel in late 1915. On Thomas MacDonagh's orders, he was replaced by Peter Paul Galligan, a Cavan native and long-standing IRB man, who was to work closely with Seamus Doyle and Seamus Rafter, the senior figures of the Wexford Brigade.

Overall command of the Volunteers in the south-east during the Rising was assigned to J. J. 'Ginger' O'Connell. Following Eoin MacNeill's countermand, O'Connell advised the Enniscorthy Volunteers to stand down. On Easter Monday, unwilling to accept this order, Galligan went to the GPO in Dublin where he met Connolly, Pearse and Plunkett.[1] As Galligan later recalled, 'Connolly instructed me to go back to Wexford as quickly as I could to mobilise the Enniscorthy Battalion and to hold the railway line to prevent troops coming through from Wexford as he expected they would be landed there. He said to reserve our ammunition and not to waste it attacking barracks or such like.'[2]

Galligan then completed a marathon 200-kilometre bicycle trip via Mulhuddart in Co. Dublin, Maynooth in Co. Kildare, and Co. Carlow in order to reach Enniscorthy without being accosted by crown forces. He finally reached the cathedral town on Wednesday evening, convened the Volunteers and told them of Connolly's instruction.

Early on Thursday morning a group of between 100 and 200 Volunteers scized the town hall and Enniscorthy Castle. They cut off the gas and water supply to the RIC barracks, which they quickly surrounded. Two civilians and an RIC constable were wounded, but otherwise there were no casualties. They also took over the Athenaeum Theatre, just up from the castle, which served as their headquarters, as well as being a temporary hospital staffed by members of Cumann na mBan.

The Volunteers were poorly armed, with only twenty rifles and 2,000 rounds of ammunition between them. However, there was no shortage of men. Hundreds from both the town and the surrounding countryside seem to have joined them very swiftly, so that by the weekend there were nearly 1,000 men; Seán Etchingham was given the task of organising the new recruits.

The approach roads to Enniscorthy were blocked with a combination of felled trees and telegraph poles. The railway station was seized, and a train bound for Arklow commandeered. Then they braced themselves for the big fight.

On Saturday a force of 1,000 British soldiers assembled at Wexford town under Lieutenant-Colonel George Arthur French, a retired army officer living locally, and the 7th Earl of Wicklow, an officer in the South Irish Horse. Meanwhile, a Volunteer cyclist arrived with Pearse's surrender. Galligan was by then manning an outpost in Ferns, Co. Wexford, but Doyle and Etchingham were so dubious about the veracity of the surrender note that, the following day, Colonel French gallantly opted to place them in a military car and escort them to Arbour Hill prison in Dublin where they could hear the word straight from the horse's mouth. Pearse confirmed the news and told Doyle that he had only surrendered because the British forces were 'shooting women and children in the streets'.[3] They duly returned to Enniscorthy where Doyle and the journalist Bob Brennan signed the surrender note, which was then formally delivered to Colonel French.

Two hundred and seventy Enniscorthy Volunteers were arrested. The leaders, including Galligan, Brennan, Doyle, Etchingham, Rafter, Richard

King and Michael de Lacy were sentenced to death, but later had their sentences commuted to imprisonment or penal servitude. As Galligan later explained to his brother, Monsignor Eugene Galligan, the Enniscorthy Volunteers fought because 'even if it was only for 12 hours … they would not stand by and watch their brothers in Dublin fall without striking a blow'.[4]

Enniscorthy-based photographer Alfred E. Crane captured this image of the Enniscorthy Volunteers being marched through the streets under armed guard. Bob Brennan is at the front wearing a grey cap, and on his left is Head Constable Collins, RIC. Seán Etchingham is directly behind Brennan, clad in a long overcoat and Volunteer slouch hat. Walking behind Etchingham are Richard King, Michael de Lacy, Seamus Doyle and Seamus Rafter.

CO. MEATH

Thomas Ashe.

Kerry-born Thomas Ashe was a schoolteacher, a passionate GAA man and a cousin of the Hollywood actor Gregory Peck. He was also a talented musician, founding the award-winning Lusk Black Raven Pipe Band.

As commandant of the 5th Battalion of the Dublin Brigade, known locally as the 'Fingal Volunteers', his force at the start of the Rising consisted of sixty poorly armed and largely untrained men. His numbers were soon depleted when James Connolly ordered him to send some of his men to the GPO. In the same orders, Ashe was instructed to raid miscellaneous local barracks and to prevent reinforcements entering the city from the north.

On Wednesday 26 April the Fingal Volunteers successfully raided RIC barracks in Swords and Donabate, confiscating weapons and ammunition. They also destroyed rail and telegraph lines. By the close of day, a number of local Volunteers from both Swords and Donabate had joined Ashe's men.

Friday 28 April was to prove Ashe's most successful day. His aim was to destroy the Midland Great Western Railway line in Batterstown to prevent British troops based in Athlone from reaching their comrades in Dublin. The route to Batterstown led the Volunteers close to Ashbourne, Co. Meath. Ashe felt that if the RIC barracks in Ashbourne was still occupied, it should be captured. Volunteer scouts duly reported that two RIC men were building a barricade outside the barracks. When a demand to surrender was answered with gunfire, a major battle ensued in which at least eight RIC officers were killed, with approximately sixteen wounded and a further thirteen captured. After five and a half hours, Ashe's men prevailed and the police surrendered. The Volunteers captured a significant quantity of arms and up to twenty vehicles. Two Volunteers and a number of civilians also died during the fight.

Following their success at Ashbourne, Ashe and his men were encamped at New Barn in Kilsallaghan, north Co. Dublin, when they received word of Pearse's surrender. Ashe's second-in-command, Richard Mulcahy, went to Dublin to verify the order, after which Ashe surrendered his battalion to the British cavalry. He was sentenced to death, but the sentence was commuted to penal servitude for life. Ashe went on to succeed Denis McCullough as president of the IRB but died as a result of being force-fed on hunger strike in Mountjoy prison in 1917, aged thirty-two.

Much of the tactical success in the capture of Ashbourne has lately been accredited to Mulcahy, who went on to become commander of the pro-Treaty forces in the Civil War after the death of Michael Collins.[5]

CO. GALWAY

Liam Mellows.

On the morning of Easter Tuesday a group of Galway Volunteers attacked the RIC barracks in the coastal village of Clarinbridge. The men were led by Liam Mellows, the twenty-four-year-old Manchester-born commandant of the Western Division (i.e. the republican forces in the west of Ireland). They entered the barracks but were driven back by the policemen, who bolted the door Another detachment of Volunteers attacked Oranmore Barracks, but again the RIC managed to barricade themselves inside before the Volunteers could capture the building.[6] A police constable called Whelan was fatally wounded during a skirmish with the rebels near Carnmore.

When the RIC district inspector got wind of the attacks, he immediately ordered the arrest of any known Sinn Féiners in Galway city, incarcerating them on an armed trawler in Galway Bay. He also recalled his men from outlying police stations, but was unable to make contact with the police in Athenry Barracks because the communication lines had already been cut.

The district inspector became particularly alarmed for the safety of the Athenry police when, following the failure to capture Oranmore, Clarinbridge or Gort Barracks, the Galway Volunteers (estimated at between 500 and 600 men) assembled at the experimental farm of the Department of Agriculture and Technical Instruction (DATI) just outside Athenry. The Athenry police were rescued later that day by a combined military, naval and police operation in which a train was commandeered for the purpose.

With no clear instructions on how to proceed, and feeling vulnerable at the DATI farm, Mellows occupied the strategically unimportant Moyode Castle on Wednesday. The following day he detailed a group of men to take up defensive positions in the cemetery at Castlegar Hill on the eastern approach to Galway city. By now the Royal Navy's 'Flower class' sloop HMS *Laburnum* was so well positioned in Galway Bay that when some suspicious motorcars began driving towards the cemetery, she was able to fire nine rounds at them, directed by a loyal observer in the cemetery. There were no reported casualties.

That same day the *Great Southern*, a requisitioned passenger ship, arrived into Galway with a contingent of Royal Munster Fusiliers, to be followed by the sloop *Snowdrop* and the cruiser *Gloucester* with more troops. With Galway now secure from attack and with increasingly glum reports from Dublin, Mellows' Volunteers began dropping away.

By Friday, with British marines encircling their position, Mellows formulated a plan to link up his remaining rebels with the Volunteers to the south in Limerick and Clare. They were on the march when word arrived of Pearse's surrender. Mellows managed to escape to the USA, but he was arrested in New York, detained without trial and charged with assisting Germany. Released in 1918, he was elected to the First Dáil as a Sinn Féin candidate for both Galway East and North Meath later that year. He helped John Devoy organise de Valera's successful fund-raising trip to the USA and became the IRA's Director of Supplies during the War of Independence. Taking a militant anti-Treaty stance during the Civil War, Mellows was executed by firing squad on 8 December 1922, in reprisal for the shooting of Free State TD Seán Hales.

HMS *Laburnum* survived until 1942, when she was scuttled during the fall of Singapore.

HMS *Laburnum*.

Denis McCullough

Born in Belfast in 1883, Denis 'Dinny' McCullough's induction
into the IRB at the age of seventeen was a somewhat inglorious
event, conducted outside a pub by a man who would clearly have
preferred to have been in the pub. Dismayed by such slothfulness,
the ambitious young piano-tuner set about revitalising the IRB in
Ulster in cahoots with Bulmer Hobson and Seán Mac Diarmada.
He took it to such extremes that he later ejected his own father
from the organisation on the grounds of drunkenness.

In 1915 he was elected president of the IRB, but he was not made aware of the Rising until just days before it was due to take place. He cautiously acceded to the plan and on Easter Monday he led 132 Volunteers and Cumann na mBan members by train from Belfast to Dungannon. The idea was to meet the Tyrone Volunteers under Pat McCartan and then to link up with Liam Mellows in Galway. However, following the confusion generated by Eoin MacNeill's countermand, McCartan's Volunteers stood down. McCullough glumly returned to Belfast, where he rounded off a bad day by shooting himself in the hand by accident. Arrested later that week, he was subsequently interned at Frongoch and imprisoned in Reading Gaol.

He resigned from the IRB after the Rising, complaining that he had been sidelined. He served as an ordinary Volunteer during the War of Independence and supported the Anglo-Irish Treaty. McCullough's wife, Agnes, was a sister of Min Ryan, who was being courted by Seán Mac Diarmada at the time of his execution.

McCullough later co-founded McCullough Pigott on Suffolk Street, Dublin, a shop famed for the manufacture and sale of traditional Irish instruments, sheet music and records. He died in Dublin in 1968.

CO. CORK

The Cork Brigade of the Irish Volunteers began training at the Volunteer Hall on Sheares Street in Cork city in January 1916. On Easter Sunday over 1,000 men from Cork city and county mobilised and travelled to various parts of the county to await further instructions, including Patrick Looney's Donoughmore Company. However, Tomás MacCurtain, commandant of the Cork Brigade, was utterly confused, having received contradictory orders from Dublin, one set from Seán Mac Diarmada saying the rebellion was on, the other from Eoin MacNeill, calling it off. That evening, he opted to stand his men down.

Members of the Donoughmore Company of the Irish Volunteers *c.* 1916. *Seated*: P. Looney and John Manning, Macroom. *Standing*: Paddy Collins-Stuake and Pat Daly, Ballycounihan, Donoughmore.

Across the Boggeragh Mountains, in Millstreet, seven Irish Volunteers paraded on Easter Sunday, armed with four single-shot .303 rifles, three shotguns, five revolvers and just over 400 rounds of ammunition.[7] They also had 100 three-pronged pikes, designed for use against cavalry horses. Although their parade also petered out, the blood was up, and Millstreet would be one of the most active rebel strongholds in Ireland during the War of Independence.

When MacCurtain learned the Rising had gone ahead in Dublin late on Easter Monday, he made his way to the Volunteer Hall in Cork city. There had been no orders from Dublin since Sunday but MacCurtain felt he needed to show some solidarity and he and his men holed up in the hall. That evening they were visited by Lord Mayor Thomas Butterfield and Bishop Daniel Cohalan, who expressed a great eagerness to forestall any bloodshed in the city. Over the next few days, these two men oversaw negotiations with the British authorities, and the Volunteers agreed to surrender their weapons on the basis that these would be returned at a later date. This agreement nearly fell apart when the details were printed in the *Constitution* newspaper, which MacCurtain felt was a clear breach of the deal. It took the diplomatic skills of both the Lord Mayor and the Bishop to convince the men to stand down.[8]

The Cork Volunteers returned home deeply dismayed that the Fates had conspired to prevent them rising up with as much vigour as the Dublin rebels had done. Many of them were arrested and detained in the Cork Military Detention Barracks over the ensuing weeks, while MacCurtain was among those transported to Dublin to be imprisoned in Richmond Barracks. He was later transferred to Reading Gaol but was released on Christmas Eve.

Cork Brigade Irish Volunteer Officers training camp at the Sheares Street Hall, Cork, in January 1916.

Front row, seated (left to right): Cornelius J. Meany, Cornelius Mahoney, Patrick J. Twomey, Martin O'Keefe, Michael Leahy, William Kelliher, James Murphy, Chris McSweeney.

Second row: Seán O'Sullivan, Christopher O'Gorman, Michael Lynch, Seán Lynch, John Manning, Charles Wall, James Walsh, Seán Carroll, Riobard Langford, Maurice Ahern, Tom Hales, Tadhg Barry, Captain J. J. 'Ginger' O'Connell.

Back row: Paud O'Donoghue, Cornelius Ahern, Seán O'Driscoll, Eugene Walsh, Denis O'Brien, Seán Collins, Seamus Courtney, Jeremiah Mullane, Michael Hyde, Liam O'Brien, Michael McCarthy.

The Kent Family

Thomas Kent, the man for whom Kent Station in Cork city is named, is often overlooked in the annals of the Easter Rising. Born in 1865, he was the second of nine children – seven sons and two daughters – raised in the Irish-speaking household of Bawnard House at Coole Lower, near Castlelyons, Co. Cork, where his parents, David and Mary Kent, ran a 200-acre farm.[9] Educated locally, he had a penchant for poetry, drama and adventure. At the age of nineteen, he emigrated to Boston, arriving just as the city elected Hugh O'Brien as its first Irish-born mayor. He spent the next five years making church furniture, as well as a stint in publishing.

Following his return to Ireland in 1889, Tom Kent became a leading member of the Castlelyons and Coolagown branch of the Irish National League. He and his brothers were frequently in court, charged with orchestrating a boycott campaign against Orr McCausland, a Belfast-based businessman who had purchased land in the area, and Robert Brown, a Scotsman who had occupied the house of an evicted neighbour. The Kents were not ones to go quietly. On one occasion the eldest brother, Edmond, shouted from the dock, 'Death or victory is our war-cry, and then the Saxon chains will break.' On another, William Kent roared, 'Victory is our cry and our motto no surrender', while Tom simultaneously slammed his fist upon the desk and shouted, 'God save Ireland.'

The Kents continued to play an active role in local politics through the 1890s and early twentieth century and were kept under near-constant police surveillance. An avid supporter of Sinn Féin and the Gaelic League, Tom Kent co-founded the Castleyons branch of the Irish Volunteers in 1913. This was said to have been the first teetotal branch of the organisation. Many of its young recruits practised their shooting in the woods around the Kents' home at Bawnard.

In August 1915 Tom attended the funeral of Jeremiah O'Donovan Rossa. Five months later he orchestrated a major disruption of a rally at Ballynoe in Co. Waterford, organised by John Redmond to recruit more Irishmen for the British Army. While Redmond spoke, Tom set up a second platform from which Terence MacSwiney, president of the Cork branch of Sinn Féin, began to speak against recruitment. Redmond's supporters were then thrown asunder by the local GAA who marched through them, carrying hurleys over their shoulders as if they were rifles.

Kent and MacSwiney were arrested for sedition under the Defence of the Realm Act (DORA). While they awaited trial, on 13 January their houses were raided. A five-chambered revolver was found at Kent's home, along with fifty-four rounds of ball cartridge and twenty-seven rounds of revolver ammunition.

The police were far more excited by a series of letters at Mac-Swiney's home on Victoria Road. These were from his brother John, who gave his address as 'Berlin'. The code-breakers set to work in a bid to prove that Sinn Féin was in open collusion with the Kaiser's spymasters. It took several weeks for them to work out that John MacSwiney lived in Berlin, Ontario.[10]

MacSwiney's trial in February was a farce. Dr H. A. Wynne, the Crown Solicitor, was a staunch unionist and pushed it too far by claiming MacSwiney had urged that 'a bullet should be put through the brain of Mr John Redmond' during his speech at Ballynoe. The magistrates dismissed the charges against MacSwiney but, adding a dash of comedy, they fined him one shilling, without costs, for being 'in possession of a cipher capable of communicating naval and military information'.[11]

Meanwhile, Tom Kent appeared before a Court of Summary Jurisdiction in Cork on 21 February, charged with making a speech at Ballynoe 'likely to cause disaffection amongst the civilian population and likely to prejudice recruiting'. The prosecutor claimed he 'played into the hands of the Germans, Turks and Bulgarians' by urging Ballynoe's inhabitants not to join 'those who were fighting their battles in France, Flanders and elsewhere'. With the exception of the stipendiary magistrate, the bench dismissed the case and he was acquitted.[12] That same day, Tom's brother Richard and a man called Kenery brazenly paraded down Fermoy's main street with a rifle, but the police appear to have turned a blind eye.

The Kent brothers were ready for action on the eve of the Rising. They spent Easter Sunday in Cork, awaiting word from Dublin to mobilise. The hours crept by, and there was still no word. Finally, a messenger arrived from Dublin with the countermanding order from MacNeill. The brothers returned to Bawnard House that evening, but all hell broke loose at 3.45 a.m. when six policemen arrived with orders to arrest the entire family. A voice from within the house retorted, 'We will never surrender – we will leave some of you dead.'[13]

As is so often the case with shoot-outs, there are several versions of what happened next.[14] Suffice it to say, a gun battle erupted in which, as British Prime Minister Herbert Asquith informed Parliament, Head Constable William Neale Rowe had his head blown off by a shot fired from a window of the house.[15]

William Kent later suggested that the fatal shot was fired by his brother Richard, who, on account of an accident, had lately spent some time in a lunatic asylum. Indeed, despite the fact that four of the Kents' guns were used, William claimed that all the shots had been fired by Richard. According to some accounts, Mrs Kent, who was in her late seventies, remained by her sons' side throughout, ensuring their guns were kept clean, cool and loaded.

At 4.50 a.m. William Kent shouted out the window that David, the youngest brother, had been hit. When he called for a priest, the police insisted that they throw down their weapons and ammunition first. Ten minutes later two shotguns were hurled from a window but no ammunition. At 6.40 a.m. the 15th Royal Fusiliers arrived and surrounded the house. With their ammunition spent, the Kents opened the door and surrendered. Thirty-six-year-old Richard Kent, an athletic man, made a bolt for the woods but was promptly shot down.[16]

The incensed constables flung Tom and William against a wall and were all set to execute them on the spot when a British officer intervened and said there had been enough shooting done. The two men were marched into Fermoy – Tom barefoot – where they were photographed on the bridge. A horse-drawn cart followed carrying their wounded brothers, David and Richard.

David and Richard were taken to Fermoy Military Hospital, where Richard died from his wounds two days later. Dr Brody at the hospital refused to allow David to face his court martial until he recovered and it was two weeks before he was transferred to Cork Military Detention Barracks. David was eventually court-martialled at Richmond Barracks, Dublin, on 14 June. He was found guilty and sentenced to death, but this was later commuted to five years' prison. He was released by Prime Minister David Lloyd George as part of a general amnesty in June 1917 and came home to a hero's welcome in Fermoy.[17] He was subsequently elected to the Executive Committee of Sinn Féin and became Sinn Féin TD for East Cork in the 1918 general election. Re-elected in 1922 as an anti-Treaty Sinn Féin TD, he continued in politics until 1927. He passed away in 1930.

Tom and William Kent appeared before a field general court martial on 4 May, charged with taking part in an armed rebellion under Regulation 50 of the DORA regulations. Explaining the trial to Westminster in July 1916, Asquith stated, 'In the interests of public safety, it was decided to exclude the public from this court, at which no counsel appeared for the prisoner.'[18]

William Kent was acquitted and went on to become the first Sinn Féin chairman of Cork County Council in 1917. From 1927 until 1933, he represented Cork East in the Dáil, initially as a Fianna Fáil TD and then with the short-lived National Centre Party. In 1934 he was awarded £1,250 compensation for the damage done to his house and furniture during the siege of Easter 1916.[19]

His brother Tom was not so lucky. Convicted of high treason, he was sentenced to death and executed in Cork Military Detention Barracks on 9 May 1916.[20] His nerves were so bad on the morning of his execution that the guards brought a chair for him to sit on. He was buried in the yard in an unmarked grave beside the barracks.

CO. DONEGAL

On Easter Sunday Daniel Kelly, Centre for the IRB in Scotland since 1909 and organiser of the Donegal Volunteers, mobilised along with six other Volunteers in his home village of Cashelnagor. The Volunteers then cycled to Creeslough, where another twenty-six men under the command of Seamus McNulty joined them. Armed with twenty-six rifles and six revolvers, they were sufficiently powerful to ward off the RIC when the police came out of their barracks to accost them. The police were told to go back inside and remain there.

'Our position was rather delicate,' explained Kelly, 'as we had no definite orders to do anything.'[21] Anticipated instructions from Pat McCartan never came, and there was ongoing puzzlement as to the meaning of Eoin MacNeill's countermand. Kelly was stationmaster of the railway at the time and was expecting to demolish some of the bridges and arches on the line.

There were still no orders on Easter Monday when he learned of 'trouble' in Dublin. Kelly and his brother Joe decided to go to the capital city without delay. However, when their train reached Portadown, Co. Armagh, they were told that no trains were going south beyond Dundalk, Co. Louth. They glumly returned home and anxiously awaited updates from Dublin.

Daniel Kelly's wife gave birth to a baby on the Wednesday. Three days later, seventeen RIC police surrounded his house in Cashelnagor and attacked his front door with boulders from his garden. As the pyjama-clad Kelly reached the bottom of the stairs to open the door, the district inspector levelled his revolver and said, 'I arrest you in connection with this Volunteer movement.'[22]

Kelly was escorted to Derry by train with an armed guard of two sergeants and four policemen and lodged in Derry Gaol along with nine other prisoners. At 6.30 a.m. the following day, the ten men were put on a train to Amiens Street Station in Dublin from where they were marched via Trinity College to Richmond Barracks. When a British soldier opined aloud, 'All these characters should be shot!', one of Kelly's armed escorts, a soldier in the Royal Inniskilling Fusiliers, responded, 'If you touch a hair on one of their heads, you will be sorry for it. These men have a country to fight for. You men have never been to war. Our battalion is only after coming from France and now we are stuck on this dirty job.'[23]

The following Friday Kelly and his fellow prisoners were placed on a ferry to Holyhead and sent to Wakefield Prison from where they were transferred to the internment camp at Frongoch.

Patrick McCartan

Born in 1878, Patrick 'Pat' McCartan was a farmer's son from Carrickmore in the heart of Co. Tyrone.[24] Educated in Monaghan, Armagh and Belfast, the energetic youngster made his way to New York in 1900 with a $10 gold piece in his pocket. He moved to Philadelphia, where he found work in a bar owned by fellow Carrickmore émigré Joe McGarrity and was initiated into Clan na Gael.[25]

In 1905 McCartan returned to Ireland and qualified as a doctor, but, effectively serving as McGarrity's man in Dublin, he retained his strong links to the republican movement and the IRB, being co-opted onto the Supreme Council in late 1914.

Among his other roles, he co-starred in the play *The Memory of the Dead* with Seán Connolly and Constance Markievicz in 1908, attended one of the first meetings of Fianna Éireann in 1909 and became editor of the journal *Irish Freedom* in 1910. During this time, he worked variously as resident surgeon in the Mater Hospital and the Cork Street Hospital in Dublin. Following a trip to the USA in 1914, he returned to Ireland with £2,000 in gold from Clan na Gael for the IRB's coffers, as well as a personal gift of £700 from McGarrity to Pearse's school, Scoil Éanna (St Enda's School).

When the idea of the Easter Rising was floated before the IRB Supreme Council in January 1916, McCartan expressed deep caution:

'We don't want any more glorious failures,' he remarked. Reflecting on the event many years later, he explained, 'I did not want our people to rush out into a revolution unprepared and without practical hope of military success. I had not then the faith in our own powers which might have been justified by later developments.'[26]

Nonetheless, sticking by his maxim that 'if one starts, we must all start', he prepared to lead the Volunteers of Tyrone into action during the Easter Rising. MacNeill's countermand in the *Sunday Independent* completely threw the men of Tyrone, but when word reached the county on Easter Monday night that the rebellion was under way in Dublin, some 500 men turned out, including a sizeable force in McCartan's rain-drenched homeland of Carrickmore. However, a police raid on their arms' depot the following day deterred the Volunteers of Donaghmore and Coalisland, who, still awaiting orders on Tuesday morning, decided to stand down.[27] McCartan was obliged to hide in a barn in the Sperrins and then went on the run. He was finally captured in February 1917 and interned in England.

From 1919 to 1921, he was Sinn Féin's representative in the USA, where he reignited his friendship with McGarrity and played a pivotal role in the evolution of the American Association for the Recognition of the Irish Republic. A reluctant supporter of the Anglo-Irish Treaty, he subsequently abandoned politics until the 1945 presidential election when, standing as an independent candidate, he won nearly 20 per cent of the vote. He was defeated by his former IRB boss, Fianna Fáil deputy leader and sitting Tánaiste, Seán T. O'Kelly. The following year he was a founding member of Seán MacBride's republican/socialist party Clann na Poblachta, serving in Seanad Éireann from 1948 to 1951. His daughter Deirdre was married to Ronnie Drew, the iconic folk singer who found fame with The Dubliners. Dr McCartan settled in Greystones, Co. Wicklow, where he died in 1963.

THE AFTERMATH OF THE
REBELLION

The Easter Rising was meticulously planned, largely by Clarke, Mac Diarmada and Plunkett, but it was foiled before it began by a double blow. The first was the failure to land 20,000 sorely needed German rifles on the Kerry coast, a disaster that culminated in the capture of Roger Casement. The second was the hasty but effective eleven-word countermand issued by Eoin MacNeill in which he overruled the orders issued covertly by the Rising's leaders and called the whole thing off. The immediate consequence of MacNeill's countermand was that only a small percentage of the 10,000 or so Irish Volunteers actually rose up in rebellion on Easter Monday.

One can but speculate about what might have happened if all the Volunteers had come out on Easter Monday. The number of British soldiers in Ireland at the time was certainly dangerously low, and perhaps a nationwide insurrection could have thrown the game wide open. If Britain's wartime cabinet had been obliged to remove any fighting men from the Western Front to tackle a rebellion in Ireland, then the implications for that ongoing stalemate with Germany may have been enormous. As it happens, they had enough men in reserve in Britain to back up the soldiers already based in Ireland. By the end of the week, much of Dublin city centre was in ruins, just like so many other European towns and cities by 1916.

At least 485 people were killed during the Easter Rising, the majority of them civilians hit by snipers, machine gun or indirect artillery fire. At least forty of the slain were children aged sixteen or under.[1] Most were caught in the crossfire, but there were occasions where civilians were deliberately killed by both loyalists and rebels. The British recorded 132 soldiers and policemen killed, mostly untested young men who ran into an ambush staged by Éamon de Valera's men at Mount Street Bridge. It's harder to gauge how many of the 2,558 rebels who 'came out' in 1916 died. Sixty-four members of the Irish Volunteers and Irish Citizen Army are said to have been killed in action, but many more may have been recorded as ordinary citizens. And, aside from all those who were killed, untold numbers of men, women and children were wounded, maimed and psychologically scarred for life.

GERMANS ADMIT FRENCH SUCCESS IN MORT HOMME FIGHT

The Daily Mirror

CERTIFIED CIRCULATION LARGER THAN THAT OF ANY OTHER DAILY PICTURE PAPER

No. 3,910.   FRIDAY, MAY 5, 1916   One Halfpenny.

ROUNDING UP THE REBELS AT DUBLIN: MANY BOYS AMONG THOSE WHO HAVE BEEN MADE PRISONER.

The front page of the *Daily Mirror* from Friday 5 May 1916, contained first-hand reports of the Rising along with news of the surrender. The paper also contained some of the first published pictures of the rebellion. Below the masthead, the caption reads: 'Rounding up the rebels at Dublin: many boys among those who have been made prisoner.' The illustrations include a photograph captioned: 'Searching a cart. Ammunition could very easily have been hidden in the straw.' Other photographs are captioned 'Soldiers stop priests in order to examine their papers' and 'Armoured car in which money was taken to the bank.'

The *Cork Free Press* of 6 May summarised the effects of the Rising while the *Sunday Pictorial* of 7 May detailed the execution of Clarke, Mac Diarmada and Plunkett. 'We do not expect that they will spare the lives of the leaders,' wrote Patrick Pearse to his mother on 1 May. The following day Pearse, Clarke and MacDonagh were subjected to a 'field general court martial' (i.e. trial without defence or jury) and, as Pearse predicted, they were sentenced to death. At dawn on 3 May, the three men were shot by firing squad in the disused Stonebreaker's Yard at Kilmainham Gaol.

In the context of the First World War, such fatality figures are low. Take, for instance, the 570 men from the 16th (Irish) Division who died when the Germans gassed the trenches at Hulluch on 27 April, the fourth day of the Rising in Dublin. Or consider the British surrender of the fortress of Kut Al Amara in Mesopotamia on the very same day Pearse surrendered in Dublin, after which 2,700 British and 6,500 Indian soldiers were taken prisoner by the Ottoman Turks. Approximately 40 per cent of the men taken captive at Kut died from disease, exposure, fatigue, mistreatment and starvation before the end of the war. Many of them were Irish.

And yet it is surely a sign of a strong society that, 100 years on, we can access the names of just about every person who died during the Easter Rising. It is hard to imagine that those rebelling against authority in the troubled zones of the modern age are blessed with such meticulous records.

Most people in Ireland strongly disapproved of the rebellion when it began. It was the disproportionate British response that ultimately led to His Majesty losing control of the vast majority of his hitherto relatively secure Irish kingdom. The antics of some of the British forces, the isolated instances of women and children being killed and, above all, the summary execution without trial of the leaders turned Ireland on its heel.

In the days that followed Pearse's surrender, 3,430 men and seventy-nine women were arrested by the authorities. Most were subsequently deemed to be of little real threat to the crown and released.[2] However, 186 men and one woman (Markievicz) were tried by court martial at Dublin's Richmond Barracks, charged with being part of a group whose actions resulted in 'casualties amongst His Majesty's troops' and, more seriously, 'with conspiracy with His Majesty's enemies'. Ninety people were sentenced to death, of whom fifteen were shot between 3 and 12 May.

Following the executions of Pearse, Clarke and MacDonagh on 3 May, John Redmond was quick to warn that 'if any more executions take place in Ireland, the position will become impossible for any Constitutional Party or leader'.[3] British Prime Minister Herbert Asquith likewise forecast that

Dulce et decorum est pro patria mori.

I nḋoıl-ċuıṁne aṙ
CONĊUƀAṘ Ó COLƀÁIRD

a ḟuaıṙ ḃáṡ aṙ ṡon na
héıṙeann

An t-oċtṁaḋ lá ʋe ƀealtaıne,
1916

Coıṙ Maṙtaṙ Éıṙeann aṙ ḃeıṙ
Dé ʒo ṙaıḃ a anam.

PRAY FOR THE SOUL OF
CORNELIUS COLBERT,
Who, with others of his fellow-patriots,
gave his life for Ireland at
Kilmainham Jail
On Monday morning, May 8th, 1916

"Greater love than this no man hath."

GILL   DUBLIN

PRAYER

BEHOLD, O good and most sweet Jesus, I cast myself upon my knees in Thy sight, and with the most fervent desire of my soul, I pray and beseech Thee that Thou wouldst impress upon my heart lively sentiments of Faith, Hope and Charity, with true repentance for my sins and a firm purpose of amendment, whilst with deep affection and grief of soul, I ponder within myself and mentally contemplate Thy Five most Precious Wounds, having before my eyes what the Prophet David put in Thy mouth concerning Thee, O good Jesus: "They have dug My hands and My feet: they have numbered all My bones."—Ps. xxi, 17, 18.

A Plenary Indulgence may be gained on the usual conditions by reciting this prayer before an image or picture of our Crucified Redeemer after Confession and Communion, and praying for the intentions of the Pope.

In Loving Memory
OF
PÁDRAIƷ MACPIARAIS
(PATRICK HENRY PEARSE)
Who gave his life for Ireland
On May 3rd, 1916
Aged 36 Years.

ALSO HIS BELOVED AND DEVOTED BROTHER
UILLIAM MACPIARAIS
(WILLIAM JAMES PEARSE)
Who gave his life in the same holy cause
On May 4th, 1916
Aged 34 Years.

ʒo nʋéanaıḋ Dıa tṙócaıṙe aṙ
n-anamnaıḃ.

O GENTLEST HEART OF JESUS, ever present in the Blessed Sacrament, ever consumed with burning love for the poor captive souls in Purgatory, have mercy on the souls of Thy servants, PATRICK and WILLIAM; bring them from the shadows of exile to the bright home of Heaven, where, we trust, Thou and Thy Blessed Mother have woven for them a crown of unfading bliss. Amen.

A MOTHER SPEAKS

Dear Mary, that didst see thy first born Son
Go forth to die amid the scorn of men
For whom He died,
Receive my two dear sons into thy arms
Who also have gone out to die for men,
And keep them by thee till I come to them,
Dear Mary, I have shared thy sorrow,
And soon shall share thy joy.

Dulce et decorum est pro patria mori.

ʒo nʋéanaıḋ Dıa na nƷṙáṡt
tṙócaıṙe aṙ anam
Éamonn Ceannt,

Ceann caṫa aṙ ṡluaʒ na nƷaeʋel
(aṙ an ʒceaṫṙaṁa caṫ)

a ṫaoıaḋ ı ʒCúıṙt aṙm Saṗana
aʒuṡ a caıṫeaḋ ı ḃṗṙıoṡún
Cıll Maıʒnean,

Dıa Luaın, 8aʋ lá ʋe ƀealtaıne,
1916

ʒo ṡaoṙaıḋ Dıa Éıṙe.

a Dıa ʒléʒıl na ṗéıle aʒuṡ a
aṫaıṙ na nʒṙáṡ,

Le ʋo naoṁṫoıl ʋo céaṗaḋ
aʒuṡ ʋo ḃṙaṫaḋ ċun ḃáıṡ,

a Aonṁıc ʋo ṡaoṙ ṡınn ó'n
ḃṗeacaḋ ṙa ṗáıṙ,

Réıʋṫıʒ na Ʒaeʋıl ḃoċta
aʒuṡ leaṙuıʒ ʒan ṙṗáṙ.

FIRST ANNIVERSARY.

I ʒCuıṁne aṙ
Seaʒan mac Ʒıolla Ḃṙıʒʋe,
MAJOR JOHN MacBRIDE,
Vice-Commandant Irish Republican Army,

Major in the Army of the South African Republic,

Organizer of the Transvaal Irish Brigade,

WHO DIED FOR IRELAND
5TH MAY, 1916.

ʒo nʋeanṙaıṙ Dıa Tṙocaıṙe aṙ
a anam.

"No man can claim authority to whittle down or barter away the immutable rights of nationhood; for Irishmen have fought, suffered, and died, through too many centuries, in defence of those rights. And, thank God, Irishmen will always be found, in the darkest and dreariest nights that fall upon our country, to snatch up the torch from the slumbering fire, to hold it up aloft as a guiding light, and to hand it on, blazing afresh, to the succeeding generation."

Major MacBride's address on the Manchester Martyrs November, 1914.

ʒo ṡaoṙaıḋ Dıa Éıṙe.

Memorial cards for Con Colbert, Patrick and Willie Pearse, Éamonn Ceannt, John MacBride and Michael O'Hanrahan (Micheál Ó hAnnrahain).

Dulce et decorum est pro patri mori.

I nḋoıl-ċuıṁne aṙ
Mıċeál Ó hAnnṙaċáın,

a ḟuaıṙ ḃáṡ aṙ ṡon na
héıṙeann

An ceaṫṙaṁaḋ lá ʋe ƀealtaıne,
1916

Coıṙ Maṙtaṙ Éıṙeann aṙ ḃeıṙ
Dé ʒo ṙaıḃ a anam.

PRAY FOR THE SOUL OF
MICHEAL O'HANNRACHAIN
Who, with others of his fellow-patriots,
gave his life for Ireland at
Kilmainham Jail
On Thursday morning, May 4th, 1916.

"Greater love hath no man than this."

PRAYER

BEHOLD, O good and most sweet Jesus, I cast myself upon my knees in Thy sight, and with the most fervent desire of my soul, I pray and beseech Thee that Thou wouldst impress upon my heart lively sentiments of Faith, Hope and Charity, with true repentance for my sins and a firm purpose of amendment, whilst with deep affection and grief soul, I ponder within myself and mentally contemplate Thy Five most Precious Wounds, having before my eyes what the Prophet David put in Thy mouth concerning Thee, O good Jesus: "They have dug My hands and My feet, they have numbered all My bones."—Ps. xxi, 17.

A Plenary Indulgence may be gained on the usual conditions by reciting this prayer before an image or picture of our Crucified Redeemer after Confession and Communion, and praying for the intentions of the Pope.

GILL   DUBLIN

excessive executions would 'sow the seeds of lasting trouble in Ireland'.[4] Despite such expressions of alarm, Sir John Maxwell, who was effectively acting as 'military governor' of Ireland at the time, did not take his foot off the accelerator. By 10 May George Bernard Shaw could no longer contain his anger. In an open letter published across the world, he wrote:

> My view is that men who were shot in cold blood after their capture or surrender were prisoners of war and it was therefore entirely incorrect to slaughter them … an Irishman resorting to arms to achieve the independence of his country is doing only what Englishmen will do if invaded and conquered by the Germans … It is absolutely impossible to slaughter a man in this position without making him a martyr and a hero, even though the day before the rising he may have been only a minor poet … The military authorities and the British Government must have known they were canonising their prisoners.[5]

Some of those who were executed appear to have been glad of such an end. Con Colbert avowed, 'We would be better off dead as life would be torture.'[6] Tom Clarke was 'relieved' because, having already spent so many long years in prison, the idea of another lengthy spell filled him with horror.

Others did not want to die. As a father of four with a pregnant wife, forty-one-year-old Michael Mallin tried to avoid the death penalty during his court martial, claiming that he was merely a tradesman and bandleader and that Constance Markievicz had been his superior officer. He was found guilty of taking part 'in an armed rebellion' and sentenced to death. He went to his execution looking 'very sad', having urged his wife, Agnes, 'to pray for all the souls who fell in this fight, Irish and English'. He became particularly emotional when thinking of his small son Joseph. 'My little man, my little man … I cannot keep the tears back when I think that he will rest in my arms no more.'[7] Joseph Mallin, who became a Jesuit priest and teacher in Hong Kong, celebrated his 101st birthday in 2014 and is the last surviving child of the men executed after the 1916 Rising.

In many ways the Easter Rising was a revolution of the old world. Among those who fought and died in 1916 were Tom Clarke and John MacBride, who were intimate with the Fenian radicals of 1867 and even with some of the veterans of the Young Ireland Rebellion of 1848. And yet there are people today who were alive when the Easter Rising broke out. As well as Fr Joe Mallin, Dorothea Findlater, who celebrated her 105th birthday in 2014, was a small girl when her father, Captain Harry de Courcy-Wheeler, accepted the surrender of Mallin and Markievicz.

The power of the Rising is that when it is whittled down to the basics, the story reads like a Hollywood epic. A band of poets and revolutionaries, men and women, posh folk and paupers, are bonded by a desire to shake off the shackles of empire. They rise up and hold out for nearly a week against impossible odds before they are defeated by a combination of superior artillery fire, armoured cars and their own moral qualms in the face of excessive civilian deaths. And then, when the empire overreacts and executes the leaders, the people of Ireland come on side in a sort of messianic second coming. It's certainly an attractive saga upon which to frame the birth of a state.

In April 1916 the Proclamation of the Republic postulated an imagined reality. And yet, within a few short years, those words had become the defining basis of a republic, albeit one that is subject to endless reinterpretation as we move ever further from the events.

Many of the men (and, to a much lesser extent, the women) who led Ireland through the War of Independence and on into the middle decades of the twentieth century were veterans of the Easter Rising. Éamon de Valera is probably the most famous, but Michael Collins, Seán T. O'Kelly, Seán McEntee and Seán Lemass all served in the GPO under Pearse and Connolly, and W. T. Cosgrave, first president of the Irish Free State, was in the South Dublin Union with Éamonn Ceannt.

There were others who were not involved in the rebellion but who became considerably more rebellious in its aftermath. Robert Barton, Director

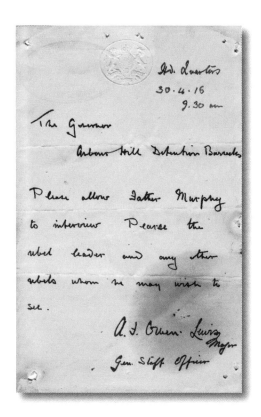

A letter written at 9.30 a.m. on Sunday 30 April, the day after Pearse's surrender, by Major A. F. Owen Lewis, general staff officer, Irish command headquarters, to the governor of the Arbour Hill Detention Barracks. It reads: 'Please allow Father [Columbus] Murphy to interview Pearse the rebel leader and any other rebels whom he may wish to see.' Major Owen Lewis gave evidence before the Hardinge Commission of Inquiry, and was later mentioned in dispatches for distinguished services during the Rising.

General Maxwell's command broadside.

PUBLIC NOTICE.

ARMS & AMMUNITION.

I, GENERAL SIR JOHN GRENFELL MAXWELL, K.C.B., K.C.M.G., C.V.O., D.S.O., Commanding in Chief His Majesty's Forces in Ireland, hereby Order that all members of the Irish Volunteer Sinn Fein Organization, or of the Citizen Army, shall forthwith surrender all arms, ammunition and explosives, in their possession to the nearest Military Authority or the nearest Police Barracks.

Any member of either of these organizations found in possession of any arms, ammunition. or explosives, after 6th May, 1916, will be severely dealt with.

J. G. MAXWELL,
GENERAL,
COMMANDING-IN-CHIEF,
THE FORCES IN IRELAND

HEADQUARTERS, IRISH COMMAND,
2nd May, 1916.

of Agriculture in the First Dáil and one of the plenipotentiaries sent to negotiate the Anglo-Irish Treaty of 1921, was in British uniform when the Rising broke out. After the surrender he was posted to Richmond Barracks, where his principal duty was to look after the personal effects of rebel prisoners, 3,000 of whom were held at the barracks before they were either released or transported to temporary detention centres in England and Scotland. Most of the men were later transferred to Frongoch internment camp in Wales.[8] By 1917 Barton had become a committed nationalist.

The Rising also transformed the political face of the nation. The repercussions of the rebellion destroyed any chance that the IPP and other constitutional nationalists could retain the upper hand in London. In the ensuing twenty months before Redmond's unexpected death, aged sixty-one, Parnell's heir could only watch helplessly as his once rock-solid support defected in their hundreds and thousands to Sinn Féin.

Arthur Griffith.

Taking its name from the Irish for 'ourselves' or 'we ourselves', Sinn Féin had been founded in 1905 by the Dublin-born journalist Arthur Griffith. In decline at the time of the Rising, authorities and newspapers alike played into the party's hand by erroneously dubbing it 'the Sinn Féin Rising'. By the time of the post-war election in 1918, Sinn Féin had become by far the most popular republican organisation in Ireland, and it swept the polls, returning seventy-three of Ireland's 105 seats, upon which was based the first Dáil Éireann or parliament of Ireland.

But perhaps the last words on the Rising should fall to Bombardier Tom Barry of the Royal Field Artillery who was serving in Mesopotamia when he caught sight of a war communiqué that was to completely alter his life. 'REBELLION IN DUBLIN' roared the headline. Barry, who was to become the most iconic guerrilla fighter in west Cork during the War of Independence, then read of the doomed Rising, the destruction of central Dublin, Pearse's surrender, the mass arrest of the Irish Volunteers and the execution of the rebel leaders. When he finished reading it, he read it again. And then he read it again and again.

'It was a rude awakening,' he recalled. 'Guns being fired at the people of my own race by soldiers of the same army with which I was serving. The echo of these guns in Dublin was to drown into insignificance the clamour of all other guns during the remaining two and a half years of war … my mind was torn with questionings. What was this Republic of which I now heard for the first time? Who were these leaders the British had executed after taking them prisoners: Tom Clarke, Padraic Pearse, James Connolly and all the others, none of whose names I had ever heard? What did it all mean? … It put me thinking. What the hell am I doing with the British Army? It's with the Irish I should be!'[9]

COPY OF LETTER OF MICHAEL MALLIN TO HIS WIFE.

My darling wife, pulse of my heart, this is the end of all things earthly sentence of death has been passed, and a quarter to four to-morrow the sentence will be carried out by shooting, and so must Irishmen pay for trying to make Ireland a free Nation. God's Will be done, I am prepared. But oh my darling if only you and the little ones were coming too, if we could all reach Heaven together, my heart strings are torn to pieces when I think of you and them, of our manly James, happy-go-lucky John, shy, warm Una, Daddy's girl, and oh little Joseph, my little man, my little man, wife, dear wife, I cannot keep back the tears when I think of him, he will rest in my arms no more. To think that I have to leave you to battle through the world with them without my help, what will you do my darling? If I had only taken your advice and left the country we might have been so happy, but Ireland always came first, but, my darling, this past fortnight has taught me that you are my only love, my only hope. With God's help I will be always near you. If you can I would like you to dedicate Una to the service of God and also Joseph so that we may have two to rest in as penance for our sins, try and do this if you can, pray to our divine Lord that it may be so. Father Mc Carthy has just been with me and heard my Confession and made me so happy and contented... God bless him... see Alderman T. Kelly, he is a good God-fearing man and will be able to help you, for my sake as well as for yours... he will know what to do, it is due to you as the wife of one of the fallen. Are you sure you left nothing

A copy of Michael Mallin's last letter to his wife.

in the house, you know the police broke in and made a thorough search?
however, these are only mere earthly things... I am so cold, this has been
such a cruel week. Mr Partrige was more than a brother to me - kept me
close in his arms so that I might have comfort and warmth. His wife is
here under arrest, if he gets out and you see him tell him that I met my
fate like a man. I do not believe that our blood has been shed in vain.
I believe that Ireland will come out greater and grander, but she must not
forget she is CATHOLIC she must keep her Faith. I find no fault with the
soldiers or police, I forgive them from the bottom of my heart, pray for
all the souls that fell in this fight, Irish and English.

God and His Blessed Mother take you and my dear ones under their
care. A husband's blessing on your dear head, my loving wife, a father's
Blessing on the heads of my children, James, John, Una, Joseph my little
man, my little man, my little man, his name unnerves me again. All your
dear faces arise before me. God Bless you God Bless you my darlings. Oh,
if you were only dying with me, but that is sinful. God and His Blessed
Mother guard you again and again, pulse of my heart, good bye for a while,
I feel you will soon be in Heaven with me. I am offering my life in atonment
for all my sins and for any debts due.

Give my love to your dear Mother, Josephine, Mr Farrell and all the
children, they must all pray for my poor soul. You will have a Mass said
for me, loved wife. My life is numbered by hours, now darling, I am drawing
nearer and nearer to God, to that Good God who died for us, you and I
love, and our children, and our children's children. God and His Blessed

Mother again and again Bless and protect you. Oh Saviour of man, if my

dear ones could die and enter Heaven with me, how Blessed and happy I

would be, they would be away from the trials and cares of the world. Una

my little one, be a nun. Joseph my little man, be a priest if you can.

James and John to you the care of your Mother, make yourselves good strong

men for her sake and remember IRELAND.

    Good bye my wife, my darling, remember me, God again Bless you and

our children.

    I must now prepare. These last few hours must be spent with God

alone.

. Your loving husband,

Michael Mallin,

Commandant,

Stephen's Green Command.

P.S.   I enclose the buttons off my sleeve. Keep them in memory of me.

N.B.   His wife often advised him to go to Australia because never strong

   in health the Irish winter used to try him very much.

Dublin Metropolitan Police Telephone.

No. of Message.   Date, 2 - 5 - 191 6

Station of Origin.   Received at_____ M.

Sent at_____ M.

From: Military Hd Qrs Parkgate St.

To: Police G Divn

Please tell the Franciscan Fathers at Church Street that the two men they wish to see at Kilmainham Detention Prison should be seen by them tonight —

A note dated 2 May 1916, from military headquarters at Parkgate Street to the Dublin Metropolitan Police, seeking the attendance of Capuchin priests at Kilmainham Gaol. The note reads: 'Please tell the Franciscan Fathers at Church Street that the two men they wish to see at Kilmainham Detention Prison should be seen by them tonight.' In the hours before their execution the following morning, Pearse, MacDonagh and Clarke were visited by the Capuchin priests, Fr Aloysius Travers, Fr Augustine Hayden and Fr Columbus Murphy.

Pearse's final letter to his mother was written in Kilmainham Gaol on the eve of his execution. 'I hope soon to see Papa,' he concluded, 'and in a little while we shall be all together again … I have not words to tell you of my love of you and how my heart yearns to you all. I will call to you in my heart at the last moment. Your son Pat.'

Last and Inspiring Address
OF
THOMAS MacDONAGH.

The sentence of the Court Martial having been conveyed to Thomas MacDonagh, he requested permission to thank the Court in person for their courtesy, and addressed them as follows:

GENTLEMEN OF THE COURT MARTIAL,

I choose to think you have but done your duty, according to your lights, in sentencing me to death. I thank you for your courtesy. It would ...

·1916·

AND never an enobled death
May Son of Ireland fear!

C.—Irish Ireland Series—(Copyright.)

IRISH REBELLION, MAY 1916.

THOMAS MacDONAGH
(Commandant of Bishop Street Area),
Executed May 3rd, 1916.
One of the signatories of the "Irish Republic Proclamation."

—receiving in return the vivifying impress of a free people. Gentlemen, you have sentenced me to death, and I accept your sentence with joy and pride, since it is for Ireland I am to die. I go to join the goodly company of the men who died for Ireland, the least of whom was worthier far than I can claim to be, and that noble band are, themselves, but a small section of the great un-numbered army of martyrs, whose Captain is the Christ who died on Calvary. Of every white-robed knight in all that goodly company we are the spiritual kin. The forms of heroes flit before my vision, and there is one, the star of whose destiny sways my own; there is one the keynote of whose nature chimes harmoniously with the swan song of my soul. It is the great Florentine, whose weapon was not the sword, but prayer and preaching. The seed he sowed fructifies to this day in God's Church. Take me away, and let my blood bedew the sacred soil of Ireland. I die in the certainty that once more the seed will fructify."

'The Last and Inspiring Address of Thomas MacDonagh', a statement purporting to be MacDonagh's address at his court martial, was circulated in the press after his trial, but its authenticity has been the subject of much debate.[10] 'Gentlemen,' he reputedly declared, 'I accept your sentence with joy and pride, since it is for Ireland I am to die ... Take me away, and let my blood bedew the sacred soil of Ireland. I die in the certainty that once more the seed will fructify.'

By December 1916 the vast bulk of those interned in the wake of the Rising had been released. However, just over 100 republicans remained in prison until June 1917 when, under immense pressure from Sinn Féin and eager to give the upcoming Irish Convention a positive start, Lloyd George, the British prime minister, announced a general amnesty for all remaining political prisoners. Huge crowds greeted the former prisoners, including Éamon de Valera, W. T. Cosgrave, Eoin MacNeill and Austin Stack, as they arrived in Dublin on 18 June. By the time they reached Westland Row (now Pearse) Station there were literally thousands waiting to cheer them home.

ENDNOTES

INTRODUCTION

1   Matthew Erin Plowman, 'Irish Republicans and the Indo-German Conspiracy of World War I', *New Hibernia Review*, 7 (3) (2003): 81–105; Glenn P. Hastedt, *Spies, Wiretaps, and Secret Operations: An Encyclopedia of American Espionage*, 2 vols, Santa Barbara, CA: ABC-CLIO, 2011, vol. I, p. 387.

2   Paul McMahon, *British Spies and Irish Rebels: British Intelligence and Ireland, 1916–45*, Woodbridge: Boydell Press, 2008, p. 261. See also Sean Cronin's *Frank Ryan: The Search for the Republic*, Dublin: Repsol Publishing, 1980; Marie V. Tarpey, 'Joseph McGarrity, Fighter for Irish Freedom', *Studia Hibernica*, 11 (1971): 164–80.

THE ORGANS OF REVOLUTION

1   Tom Doyle, *The Civil War in Kerry*, Cork: Mercier Press, 2008, p. 16.

2   A letter written by Michael Collins from Frongoch internment camp, quoted in Donal Fallon's *The Pillar*, Dublin: New Island, 2014, p. 54.

3   John O'Leary, *Recollections of Fenians and Fenianism*, London: Downey & Co., 1896, vol. I, p. 84.

4   F. S. L. Lyons, *Ireland since the Famine*, London: Fontana, 1973, p. 315.

5   *Ibid.*, pp. 318–19.

6   Marnie Hay, *Bulmer Hobson and the Nationalist Movement in Twentieth-Century Ireland*, Manchester: Manchester University Press, 2009.

7   *Ibid.*, p. 69.

8   Two trade unionists, John Byrne and James Nolan, were beaten to death. Seumas Kavanagh, a member of the Fianna, recalled, 'One of our Fianna boys, Patsy O'Connor, got a smack of a baton on the head, as a result of which he died subsequently.' Seumas Kavanagh, BMH WS 1670, p. 10; available at http://www.bureauofmilitaryhistory.ie/reels/bmh/BMH.WS1670.pdf (accessed 17 January 2015).

9   By White's own account, he first proposed the ICA at a meeting of the Civic League (a group of intellectuals, artists and academics that included Robin Gwynn, George Russell, Padraic Colum, Francis Sheehy-Skeffington and a 'very drunk' Tom Kettle). This took place in Gwynn's room at Trinity College. White said that he conceived of the Citizen Army as a practical way of putting his military skills to use while still keeping his pacifism intact. Connolly's own writings suggest that it was he who initiated the idea and that White's appearance in the strikers' camp was merely fortuitous. See Leo Keohane, *Captain Jack*

White: Imperialism, Anarchism and the Irish Citizen Army, Dublin: Merrion Press, 2014, p. 100.

10 A list of the names of the women of the Irish Citizen Army is available at http://irishvolunteers.org/2013/08/mary-devereux-mrs-allen-irish-citizen-armygarrison-of-st-stephens-greencollege-of-surgeons (accessed 17 January 2015).

11 The Army Council also included James Larkin, P. T. Daly, Councillor William Partridge and Thomas Foran.

12 Lyons, *Ireland since the Famine*, p. 285.

13 Keohane, *Captain Jack White*, p. 134.

14 *Ibid*, p. 178.

15 *Ibid*, p. 182.

16 David Krause (ed.), *The Letters of Sean O'Casey: 1942–54*, London: Macmillan, 1975, p. 24.

17 James Connolly, *Workers' Republic*, 30 October 1915.

18 Interview with Helena Molony, aired in *Irish Women Revolutionaries, Part 3*, available at https://www.youtube.com/watch?v=R7A_csCT4jg (accessed 17 January 2015).

19 Frank Daly and Eamonn Dore, the two Volunteers who escorted Connolly, were assigned the duty by Commandant Ned Daly as Dolphin's Barn fell within his area of operations. Connolly was absent from Liberty Hall for three days and some thought he had been kidnapped. There has been considerable speculation about his absence over the years, but the ICA later stated that it was a prearranged meeting. See Paul O'Brien, *Shootout: The Battle for St Stephen's Green, 1916*, Dublin: New Island, 2013, p. xii; and Chapter 35 in Donal Nevin, *James Connolly, a Full Life: A Biography of Ireland's Renowned Trade Unionist and Leader of the 1916 Easter Rising*, Dublin: Gill & Macmillan, 2006.

20 See 'Sean O'Casey and the 1916 Rising: A Prisoner in 'the Merchants', and a 'Cup of Scald', available at http://eastwallforall.ie/?p=2322 (accessed 17 January 2015).

21 John O'Beirne Ranelagh states that within weeks of the formation of the UVF in January 1913, General Sir George Richardson was drilling over 100,000 men. By September 1914, around the time of Redmond's Woodenbridge speech, the Irish Volunteers had a force of about 180,000 men. See John O'Beirne Ranelagh, *A Short History of Ireland*, 3rd edn, Cambridge University Press, 2012, pp. 184 and 193.

22 Owen McGee, *The IRB: The Irish Republican Brotherhood from the Land League to Sinn Féin*, Dublin: Four Courts Press, 2005, pp. 353–4.

23 Michael Foy and Brian Barton, *The Easter Rising*, Stroud: Sutton Publishing, 2004, pp. 7–8.

24 Lyons, *Ireland since the Famine*, p. 341.

25 Michael Tierney, *Eoin MacNeill: Scholar and Man of Action, 1867–1945*, Oxford: Clarendon Press, 1980, p. 141.

26 Diarmuid Lynch, *The I.R.B. and the 1916 Insurrection*, ed. Florence O'Donoghue, Cork: Mercier Press, 1957, p. 96.

27 'Covenant to Indemnify the Ulster Volunteers', *Orange Sentinel*, 26 March 1914, p. 136. Quoted in Robert McLaughlin, *Irish Canadian Conflict and the Struggle for Irish Independence, 1912–25*, Toronto: University of Toronto Press, 2013; available at books.google.com.

28 The women of Inghinidhe na hÉireann also taught Irish language, music, dancing and history.

29 Elizabeth Coxhead, *Daughters of Erin: Five Women of the Irish Renaissance*, London: Secker & Warburg, 1965, p. 44.

30 Karen Margaret Steele, *Women, Press, and Politics during the Irish Revival*, New York: Syracuse University Press, 2007, p. 149. Delia Larkin's remarks were published in her inaugural column in the *Irish Worker*.

31 Cumann na mBan manifesto (1914), in Angela Bourke (ed.), *The Field Day Anthology of Irish Writing*, vol. V: *Irish Women's Writing and Traditions*, Cork: Cork University Press, 2005, p. 104.

32 Lil Conlon, *Cumann na mBan and the Women of Ireland 1913–25*, Kilkenny: Kilkenny People, 1969, p. 13.

33 Joseph McKenna, *Guerrilla Warfare in the Irish War of Independence, 1919–21*, Jefferson, NC: McFarland, 2011, p. 111.

34 Kathleen Clarke, *Kathleen Clarke: Revolutionary Woman*, ed. Helen Litton, Dublin: The O'Brien Press, 2008, p. 100.

35 Richard Londraville and Jane Londraville, *Too Long a Sacrifice: The Letters of Maud Gonne and John Quinn*, Selinsgrove, PA: Susquehanna University Press, 1999, p. 155.

36 Elizabeth Keane, *Seán MacBride, a Life: From IRA Revolutionary to International Statesman*, Dublin: Gill & Macmillan, 2007, p. 30.

37 Geoffrey Elborn, *Francis Stuart: A Life,* Dublin: Raven Arts Press, 1990, p. 236.

38 Elaine Sisson, *Pearse's Patriots: St Enda's and the Cult of Boyhood*, Cork: Cork University Press, 2005, pp. 123–4.

39 Marnie Hay, 'The Foundation and Development of Na Fianna Éireann, 1909–16', *Irish Historical Studies*, 36 (141) (2008): 53–71, at p. 55.

40 *Ibid.*, pp. 57–8. It is not certain what Markievicz's position was. Some refer to the election of her and Pádraig Ó Riain as joint secretaries, while others suggest that Markievicz became vice-president and Ó Riain secretary.

41 *Ibid.*, p. 59.

42 From a 1914 anti-Home Rule propaganda poster/pamphlet by the Unionist Association of Ireland. Reprinted in Éamon Martin, '"The Irish National Boy Scouts – A School For Rebels" – The Unionist Association', available at https://fiannaeireannhistory.wordpress.com/2014/10/06/fianna-eireann-and-anti-home-rule-propaganda (accessed 17 January 2015).

43 Éamon Martin, BMH WS 591, p. 10; available at http://www.bureauofmilitaryhistory.ie/reels/bmh/BMH.WS0591.pdf (accessed 17 January 2015).

44 Garry Holohan (aka Gearoid Ua h-Uallachain), BMH WS 328, p. 40; available at http://www.bureauofmilitaryhistory.ie/reels/bmh/BMH.WS0328.pdf (accessed 17 January 2015).

45 The following Fianna members were killed in action during Easter Week: Brendan Donelan (24 April), Seán Healy (24 April), James Fox (25 April), James Kelly (25 April), Gerald Keogh (27 April), Seán Howard (27 April) and Frederick Ryan (27 April). Donelan is listed as being from Galway, while the others were based in Dublin. ('Fianna Roll of Honour' in Robert Holland, *A Short History of Fianna Éireann*, 14 August 1949, p. 25 (NLI, MS 35,455/3/12A). Quoted in Hay, 'The Foundation and Development of Na Fianna Éireann', p. 69.

46 Hay, 'The Foundation and Development of Na Fianna Éireann', p. 69.

47 Ruth Dudley Edwards, *Speaking Ill of the Dead: Countess Markievicz*, recorded in March 2006 by RTÉ Radio.

48 A lecture to the IWFL in 1915, quoted in Maedhbh McNamara and Paschal Mooney, *Women in Parliament: Ireland, 1918–2000*, Dublin: Wolfhound Press, 2000.

49 'The Count, Stasco, Mrs Skeff, M. O'Byrne, Emer, Mrs & May Coughlan, D. Cavanagh & I were with her. Dev came later. We each got one of her roses.' Extract from the unpublished diary of Dr Kathleen Lynn, 14 July 1927, transcribed by Pat Quigley and held by the Allen Library, Dublin.

50 Letter to Josslyn Gore-Booth, 17 October 1916, Lissadell Papers, PRONI, D4131.

51 Pádraig Óg Ó Ruairc, 'A Short History of the Hibernian Rifles, 1912–16', TheIrishStory. com, 31 March 2013. Available at www.theirishstory.com/2013/03/31/a-short-history-of-the-hibernian-rifles-1912–1916/#.VNu7I8ZmlsZ (accessed 18 February 2015).

52 *Ibid.*

53 *Ibid.*

54 Seán O'Mahony, *Frongoch: University of Revolution*, Killiney: FDR Teoranta, 1987, p. 26.

55 Ó Ruairc, 'A Short History'.

56 Desmond FitzGerald, *Desmond's Rising: Memoirs 1913 to Easter 1916*, Dublin: Liberties Press, 2006, pp. 142–4.

PREPARING FOR REBELLION

1 David Lloyd George, *War Memoirs*, London: Odhams, 1924, vol. I, p. 32.

2 Tierney, *Eoin MacNeill*, pp. 171–2.

3 T. M. Kettle and Mary Kettle (eds), *The Ways of War*, Dublin: Talbot Press, 1917, p. 4.

4 *Ibid.*, p. 69.

5 'News from Ireland: An Appeal to Irishmen', *The Tablet*, 7 August 1915. Available at http://archive.thetablet.co.uk/article/7th-august-1915/18/news-from-ireland (accessed 18 February 2015).

6 Kettle and Kettle, *The Ways of War*, p. 32.

7 León Ó Bróin, *Protestant Nationalists in Revolutionary Ireland: The Stopford Connection*, Dublin: Gill & Macmillan, 1985, p. 117.

8 Letter from T. M. Kettle to Sir Henry McLaughlin, 7 August 1916, McLaughlin Papers, PRONI D.3809/67/2. Quoted in Timothy Bowman, *Irish Regiments in the Great War: Discipline and Morale*, Manchester: Manchester University Press, 2006, p. 128.

9 Speech at the grave of O'Donovan Rossa (1 August 1915) by Patrick Pearse. Published by the Office of Public Works, Dublin. Available at http://www.thefullwiki.org/Speech_at_the_Grave_of_O'Donovan_Rossa (accessed 18 February 2015).

10 James Pearse's first wife, Emily Susanna Fox, died aged thirty in 1876, leaving him with two children. Three more children from his first marriage died in infancy. For more, see Brian Crowley, 'The Strange Thing I Am: His Father's Son', *History Ireland*, 14 (2) (2006).

11 R. E. Foster, *Vivid Faces: The Revolutionary Generation in Ireland, 1890–1923*, London: Allen Lane, 2014, p. 135.

12 Angus Mitchell, *Sir Roger Casement's Heart of Darkness: The 1911 Documents*, Dublin: Irish Manuscripts Commission, 2003, p. 386.

13 *Ibid.*, p. 536.

14 Florence Monteith Lynch, *The Mystery Man of Banna Strand: The Life and Death of Captain Robert Monteith*, New York: Vantage Press, 1959, p. 121.

15 'Killorglin during the 1916 Rising', Killorglin Archive Society, available at http://killorglinarchives.com/?p=6221 (accessed 17 January 2015).

16 In recent years, Lynch's role has been brought to light again by Eileen McGough's book *Diarmuid Lynch: A Forgotten Irish Patriot*, Cork: Mercier Press, 2013. Much of the information in this section came from that book.

17 Christopher Brady, BMH WS 705, p. 6; available at http://www.bureauofmilitaryhistory.ie/reels/bmh/BMH.WS0705.pdf (accessed 17 January 2015).

18 Robert K. Massie, *Castles of Steel*, New York: Random House, 2003, p. 558.

19 Brian Barton, *From Behind a Closed Door: Secret Court Martial Records of the 1916 Easter Rising*, Belfast: Blackstaff Press, 2002, p. 295.

DUBLIN RISES

1 On 1 May 1959 Éamon Martin delivered a lecture to the Association of the Old Dublin Brigade at 51 Parnell Square entitled 'The Capture of the Magazine Fort in 1916'. He stated that they had about twenty men altogether, not thirty. Other accounts say about seventeen men.

2 Patrick O'Daly, BMH WS 220, p. 4; available at http://www.bureauofmilitaryhistory.ie/reels/bmh/BMH.WS0220.pdf (accessed 28 April 2015).

3 Éamon Martin, BMH WS 592, p. 1; available at http://www.bureauofmilitaryhistory.ie/reels/bmh/BMH.WS0592.pdf (accessed 28 April 2015).

4 Patrick O'Daly, BMH WS 220, p. 7.

5 Marlborough Barracks was home to the 6th Reserve Cavalry Regiment comprising a mixed troop of 9th and 12th Lancers, as well as the 3/1st City of London Yeomanry (Rough Riders) and the 3/1st County of London Yeomanry (Sharpshooters).

6 Garry Holohan, BMH WS 328, p. 60.

7 George Alexander Playfair died of his wounds on 29 April 1916. His death is recorded in the Irish War Memorial, indicating that he may have been in the British Army Reserves. The matter became subject to considerable controversy when a story circulated that the dead boy was the Playfairs' fourteen-year-old son, Gerald. Gerald was neither shot nor wounded but moved to Canada, where he was married in Toronto in 1923. Major Playfair, his father, was posted to Sierra Leone in July 1922 and died of heart failure the following month. For more, see Joe Duffy, 'Children of the Revolution', *History Ireland*, 21 (3) (2013), available at www.historyireland.com/20th-century-contemporary-history/children-of-the-revolution (accessed 18 February 2015); or listen to Joe Duffy, 'How a 1916 Myth Lives On', *The History Show*, RTÉ Radio 1, 24 March 2013. See also Johnny Doyle's study of the Playfairs, 'Major George Robert Playfair MC', available at http://johnny-doyle.blogspot.ie/2013/03/major-george-robert-playfair-mc.html (accessed 17 January 2015).

8 *The Irish Times*, 25 April 1916.

9 Martin, 'The Capture of the Magazine Fort in 1916' (see note 1 above).

10 Helen Litton, *16 Lives: Edward Daly*, Dublin: The O'Brien Press, 2013, p. 35.

11 Seán McGarry, BMH WS 368, p. 19; available at http://www.bureauofmilitaryhistory.ie/reels/bmh/BMH.WS0368.pdf (accessed 17 January 2015).

12 Mick O'Farrell, *The 1916 Diaries of an Irish Rebel and a British Soldier*, Cork: Mercier Press, 2014, p. 183.

13 Stephen Ferguson, *The GPO: 200 Years of History*, Cork: Mercier Press, 2014, p. 126.

14 Stephen Ferguson, *GPO Staff in 1916: Business as Usual*, Cork: Mercier Press, 2012, p. 52.

15 *The Irish Times*, 13 May 1916, quoted in Fallon, *The Pillar*, p. 57.

16 Foy and Barton, *The Easter Rising*, pp. 139–40.

17   *Ibid.*, p. 267.

18   Michael Staines, BMH WS 284, p. 13; available at http://www.bureauofmilitaryhistory.ie/reels/bmh/BMH.WS0284.pdf (accessed 28 April 2015).

19   Lorcan Collins, *16 Lives: James Connolly*, Dublin: The O'Brien Press, 2013, p. 288.

20   Notes on the Shields Family Archive, James Hardiman Library, NUIG. Available at http://archives.library.nuigalway.ie/col_level.php?col=T13 (accessed 18 February 2015).

21   'Arthur Shields Remembers the Abbey', in E. H. Mikhail (ed.), *The Abbey Theatre: Interviews and Recollections*, Lanham, MD: Rowman & Littlefield, 1988, p. 157.

22   Daire Brunicardi, *Haulbowline: The Naval Base and Ships of Cork Harbour*, Dublin: The History Press, 2012, pp. 124–5.

23   Liz Gillis, *Women of the Irish Revolution*, Cork: Mercier Press, 2014, p. 14.

24   Lar Joye, 'TSS *Helga II*', *History Ireland*, 18 (2) (2010).

25   Keohane, *Captain Jack White*, pp. 3 and 108.

26   Fearghal McGarry, *Rebels: Voices from the Easter Rising*, London: Penguin, 2011, p. 146.

27   *Ibid.*, p. 363.

28   Barton, *From Behind a Closed Door*.

29   Charles Townshend, *Easter 1916: The Irish Rebellion*, London: Penguin, 2006, p. 293.

30   Las Fallon, *Dublin Fire Brigade and the Irish Revolution*, Dublin: South Dublin Libraries, 2012, p. 60.

31   Litton, *16 Lives: Edward Daly*, p. 39.

32   *Ibid.*

33   *Ibid.*

34   P. J. Stephenson, 'Heuston's Fort', April 1966, available at www.1916-rising.com/3-heustonsfort.html (accessed 6 February 2015).

35   Desmond Ryan, *The Rising: The Complete Story of Easter Week*, Dublin: Golden Eagle Books, 1966, pp. 162–3.

36   Anne-Marie Ryan, *16 Dead Men: The Easter Rising Executions*, Cork: Mercier Press, 2014, pp. 141, 163.

37   The Parliamentary Debates (Official Report): House of Commons, HM Stationery Office, 3 May 1916, vol. 82.

38   Maurice Curtis, *The Liberties: A History*, Dublin: The History Press, 2013, chapter 11.

39   Shane Kenna, *16 Lives: Thomas MacDonagh*, Dublin: The O'Brien Press, 2014, p. 232.

40   *Ibid.*, p. 237.

41   Seosamh de Brun, BMH WS 312, p. 18; available at http://www.bureauofmilitaryhistory.ie/reels/bmh/BMH.WS0312.pdf (accessed 28 April 2015).

42   Kenna, *16 Lives: Thomas MacDonagh*, p. 259.

43   *Ibid.*, p. 259.

44   Keane, *Seán MacBride*, p. 6.

45   Maud Gonne, *The Gonne–Yeats Letters, 1893–1938*, Syracuse, NY: Syracuse University Press, 1994, p. 168. As it happens, the governor of Gibraltar at this time was Sir George White, father of Jack White, first commandant of the Irish Citizen Army.

46   Keane, *Seán MacBride*, p. 25.

47   J. B. Lyons, *The Enigma of Tom Kettle: Irish Patriot, Essayist, Poet, British Soldier*, Dublin: Glendale Press, 1983, p. 294; Keane, *Seán MacBride*, p. 26.

48 Quinn to Gonne, 29 July 1916, quoted in Londraville and Londraville, *Too Long a Sacrifice*, p. 272; Keane, *Seán MacBride*, p. 26.

49 Jason McElligott, 'In the Line of Fire', *History Ireland*, 20 (3) (2012): 44–5.

50 Conor Kostick, *16 Lives: Michael O'Hanrahan*, Dublin: The O'Brien Press, 2015. Available at books.google.com.

51 His brother Harry was imprisoned in Portland, Dorset, for his role in the Rising. Released in the amnesty of 1917, he was rearrested without charge in 1920 and taken to Wormwood Scrubs, where he participated in a hunger strike alongside the other republican prisoners. He died on 20 September 1927. The O'Hanrahan sisters were all active members of Cumann na mBan. The youngest brother, Edward, had a job in the Post Office at Carlow where he stayed when the rest moved to Dublin around 1902.

52 Townshend, *Easter 1916*, p. 173.

53 James Coughlan, BMH WS 304, p. 16; available at http://www.bureauofmilitaryhistory.ie/reels/bmh/BMH.WS0304.pdf (accessed 28 April 2015).

54 Foy and Barton, *The Easter Rising*, p. 135.

55 Paul O'Brien, *Uncommon Valour: 1916 and the Battle of the South Dublin Union*, Cork: Mercier Press, 2010, p. 102.

56 Thomas J. Morrissey, *William O'Brien 1881–1968: Socialist Republican, Dáil Deputy, Editor, and Trade Union Leader*, Dublin: Four Courts Press, 2007, p. 106.

57 Shane Hegarty and Fintan O'Toole, *The Irish Times Book of the 1916 Rising*, Dublin: Gill & Macmillan, 2006, p. 164.

58 Statement by Éamonn Ceannt written in Kilmainham Gaol, 7 May 1916, Cell 88. Quoted by Piaras F. Mac Lochlain, *Last Words: Letters and Statements of the Leaders Executed after the Rising at Easter, 1916*, Dublin: Kilmainham Jail Restoration Society, 1971, p. 136.

59 Seán Heuston and Éamonn Ceannt were also educated by the Christian Brothers of North Richmond Road, as were Seán Lemass, Seán T. O'Kelly, Tom Kettle and Emmet Dalton. Indeed, 125 past pupils from the school are believed to have fought in the Easter Rising. Seán Boyne, *Emmet Dalton: Somme Soldier, Irish General, Film Pioneer*, Dublin: Merrion Press, 2014, p. 9.

60 Foster, *Vivid Faces*, p. 128.

61 Michael Laffan, *Judging W. T. Cosgrave*, Dublin: Royal Irish Academy Press 2014.

62 John O'Callaghan, *16 Lives: Con Colbert*, Dublin: The O'Brien Press, 2015.

63 Ernie O'Malley, *On Another Man's Wound: Personal History of Ireland's War of Independence*, Lanham, MD: Rowman & Littlefield, 2001, p. 39.

64 R. M. Fox, *History of the Irish Citizen Army*, Dublin: James Duffy & Co., 1943, pp. 227–8.

65 Max Caulfield, *The Easter Rebellion*, 2nd edn, Dublin: Gill & Macmillan, 2014, p. 319.

66 Geraldine Fitzgerald, extracts from her personal diary, 24 April 1916 (WO 35/207), quoted by Ann Matthews in *Renegades: Irish Republican Women 1900-1922*, Cork: Mercier Press, 2010, p. 129.

67 Ann Matthews, *The Irish Citizen Army*, Cork: Mercier Press, 2014, p. 98.

68 Rose Hackett, BMH WS No. 546, p. 5; available at http://www.bureauofmilitaryhistory.ie/reels/bmh/BMH.WS0546.pdf (accessed 28 April 2015).

69 *Ibid.*, p. 8.

70 *Ibid.*, p. 5.

71 *Ibid.*, p. 8.

72 *Ibid.*, p. 10.

73 Ella Webb's photograph was originally printed in *The Sinn Féin Rebellion Handbook*, published by *The Irish Times* in 1916.

74 Peter Somerville Large, *Irish Voices: An Informal History, 1916–66*, London: Pimlico, 2000, p. 4.

75 Declan Kiberd, *1916 Rebellion Handbook*, Dublin: Mourne River Press, 1998, p. 232.

76 Obituary, *The Irish Times*, 4 September 1944.

77 Jim Herlihy, *The Dublin Metropolitan Police: A Short History and Genealogical Guide*, Dublin: Four Courts Press, 2001, p. 175.

78 Some of the rooms at the Castle were converted into makeshift hospital wards. Among the wounded who lay there was James Connolly, who was kept at the Castle before his execution in Kilmainham Gaol.

79 Matthews, *The Irish Citizen Army*, pp. 91, 110.

80 Sinéad McCoole, *No Ordinary Women: Irish Female Activists in the Revolutionary Years 1900–1923*, Dublin: The O'Brien Press, 2008, p. 45.

81 Richard Ellman (ed.), *Letters of James Joyce*, vol. II, New York: Viking, 1966, p. 81.

82 Francis Sheehy-Skeffington and Hanna Sheehy-Skeffington, *A Forgotten Small Nationality: Ireland and the War*, New York: Donnelly Press, 1916, p. 16.

83 Sean O'Casey, *The Story of the Citizen Army*, Dublin: Maunsel & Co., 1919, p. 64.

84 Foy and Barton, *The Easter Rising*, p. 117.

85 Seamus Doyle, BMH WS 166, p. 6; available at http://www.bureauofmilitaryhistory.ie/ reels/bmh/BMH.WS0166.pdf (accessed 28 April 2015).

86 Caulfield, *The Easter Rebellion*, p. 221.

87 John Evelyn Wrench, *Struggles, 1914–20*, London: Ivor Nicholson & Watson, 1935, pp. 205–6.

88 *Ibid.*, p. 206.

89 Before the fighting started Malone sent home two young Volunteers, Paddy Byrne and Michael Rowe, who had been with him, as he feared for their safety in the imminent fighting.

90 The battle inspired the acclaimed 2013 docudrama *A Terrible Beauty*, produced by Tile Films. The details are also brilliantly covered in Paul O'Brien's 2008 book, *Blood on the Streets: 1916 and the Battle of Mount Street Bridge*, Cork: Mercier Press.

91 Barry Kennerk, *Moore Street: The Story of Dublin's Market District*, Cork: Mercier Press, 2012, p. 66; Caulfield, *The Easter Rebellion*, p. 355.

92 Tim Horgan, *Dying for the Cause: Kerry's Republican Dead*, Cork: Mercier Press, 2015, pp. 405–6.

93 Joe Good, *Enchanted by Dreams: The Journal of a Revolutionary*, Dingle: Brandon Press, 1996; Aodogán O'Rahilly, *Winding the Clock: O'Rahilly and the 1916 Rising*, Dublin: Lilliput Press, 1991.

94 Letters from The O'Rahilly to his wife and son. National Library of Ireland MS 21,854.

95 Aodogán O'Rahilly, *Winding the Clock: O'Rahilly and the 1916 Rising*, Dublin: Lilliput Press, 1991, p. 223.

96 John Loder, *Hollywood Hussar: The Life and Times of John Loder*, Wimbledon: Howard Baker, 1977, p. 42. Loder confusingly claims Pearse gave his possessions to the priest to pass onto his 'wife', but Pearse was not married.

1   Dorney, John, 'The Easter Rising in County Wexford, www.theirishstory.com, 10 April 2012.

2   Peter Paul Galligan, BMH WS 170, p. 7; available at http://www.bureauofmilitaryhistory. ie/reels/bmh/BMH.WS0170.pdf (accessed 28 April 2015).

3   Seamus Doyle, BMH WS 315, p. 14; available at http://www.bureauofmilitaryhistory.ie/ reels/bmh/BMH.WS0315.pdf (accessed 28 April 2015).

4   Peter Paul Galligan to Monsignor Eugene Galligan, 29 November 1917. Quoted by John Dorney in 'The Easter Rising in County Wexford', www.theirishstory.com, 10 April 2012.

5   Foy and Barton, *The Easter Rising*, p. 283.

6   Brunicardi, *Haulbowline*, pp. 126–8; McGarry, *Rebels*, chapter 6.

7   The seven Volunteers were Cornelius Healy, Cornelius J. Meaney, Seamus Hickey, Jeremiah Twomey, Daniel A. Hickey, Michael Riordan and Patrick O'Sullivan.

8   Fionnuala Mac Curtain, *Remember … It's for Ireland: A Family Memoir of Tomás Mac Curtáin*, Cork: Mercier Press, 2006, p. 79.

9   It is to be noted that *The Irish Times* of 10 July 1867 (p. 3) refers to the arrest of a Fenian called David Kent for 'suspicion of connection with the recent rising'.

10 P. S. O'Hegarty, *A Short Memoir of Terence MacSwiney*, Dublin: Talbot Press, 1922, pp. 62–4.

11 *Ibid.*, pp. 62–4.

12 *The Irish Times*, 16 February 1916, p. 7; 29 February 1916, p. 3 (the latter date is too faded to read); *Weekly Irish Times*, 29 April 1916, p. 7.

13 'Sinn Féin Rebellion Handbook, Easter, 1916', compiled by the *Weekly Irish Times*, Dublin, 1917, p. 126.

14 Probably the most detailed account of the siege is on page 2 of the *Weekly Irish Times*, 24 June 1916.

15 'Questions in Parliament: The Case of Tomas Kent', *The Irish Times*, 6 July 1916, p. 6.

16 Asquith told Parliament that Richard 'was shot while attempting to escape after the surrender'; *Ibid.*

17 *The Irish Times*, 26 June 1917, p. 5.

18 'Questions in Parliament: The Case of Tomas Kent', *The Irish Times*, 6 July 1916, p. 6.

19 *The Irish Times*, 20 July 1934, p. 7.

20 *Weekly Irish Times*, 29 April 1916, p. 7.

21 Daniel Kelly, BMH WS 1004, p. 17; available at http://www.bureauofmilitaryhistory.ie/ reels/bmh/BMH.WS1004.pdf (accessed 28 April 2015).

22 *Ibid.*, p. 18.

23 Liam Ó Duibhir, *The Donegal Awakening: Donegal and the War of Independence*, Cork: Mercier Press, 2009, p. 42.

24 Patrick McCartan, BMH WS 766; available at www.bureauofmilitaryhistory.ie/reels/bmh/ BMH.WS0766.pdf (accessed 17 January 2015).

25 M. J. Kelly, *The Fenian Ideal and Irish Nationalism, 1882–1916*, Woodbridge: Boydell & Brewer, 2006, pp. 179–91.

26 McCartan, BMH WS 766, p. 41.

27 Sean McMahon, *Rebel Ireland: Easter Rising to Civil War*, Cork: Mercier Press, 2001, pp. 40–1.

THE AFTERMATH OF THE REBELLION

1 Duffy, 'Children of the Revolution'.

2 Hegarty and O'Toole, *The Irish Times Book of the 1916 Rising*, pp. 160–1.

3 Townshend, *Easter 1916*, p. 280. John Dillon, another prominent parliamentarian, likewise warned that 'it really would be difficult to exaggerate the amount of mischief the executions are doing'. Hegarty and O'Toole, *The Irish Times Book of the 1916 Rising*, p. 161.

4 Hegarty and O'Toole, *The Irish Times Book of the 1916 Rising*, p. 161.

5 Also published in the *Cornell Daily Sun*, 11 May 1916, available at http://cdsun.library.cornell.edu/cgi-bin/cornell?a=d&d=CDS19160511.2.14# (accessed 6 February 2015).

6 Hegarty and O'Toole, *The Irish Times Book of the 1916 Rising*, p. 168.

7 Sinéad McCoole, *Easter Widows*, New York: Random House, 2014, p. 257.

8 Liam Ó Duibhir in *Prisoners of War: Ballykinlar Internment Camp 1920-1921* (Mercier Press, 2013), p. 19, states: 'In the aftermath of the 1916 Rising, 3,226 men and seventy-seven women were arrested. A total of 1,862 men and five women were served with internment orders under Regulation 14(b) of the Defence of the Realm Act 1914. They were transferred to Britain and temporarily held in various detention centres in England and Scotland, including Knutsford, Stafford, Wakefield, Wandsworth, Woking, Lewes, Barlinnie prison in Glasgow and Perth. Some of the internees served their terms of detention in English jails, but the vast majority of the male internees were transferred to the Frongoch internment camp, near Bala in North Wales.'

9 Tom Barry, *Guerilla Days in Ireland*, Cork: Mercier Press, 2013, pp. 17–18.

10 Kenna, *Thomas MacDonagh*, pp. 248–50.

BIBLIOGRAPHY

Thanks to the miracle of the Internet, much of the research for this book was conducted at home, using such wonderful online resources as the witness statements from the Bureau of Military History at the Military Archives as well as the *Irish Times* Digital Archive, Irish newspaper archives, the Public Records Office of Northern Ireland, the National Archives of Ireland's 1901 and 1911 censuses, the Irish Architectural Archive and Google Books. I must also give a nod to my Facebook followers on Wistorical.

BOOKS AND ARTICLES

Barry, Tom, *Guerrilla Days in Ireland*, Cork: Mercier Press, 2013

Barton, Brian, *From Behind a Closed Door: Secret Court Martial Records of the 1916 Easter Rising*, Belfast: Blackstaff Press, 2002

Bateson, Ray, *They Died by Pearse's Side*, Dublin: Irish Graves Publications, 2010

Bourke, Angela (ed.), *The Field Day Anthology of Irish Writing*, vol. V: *Irish Women's Writing and Traditions*, Cork: Cork University Press, 2005

Bowman, Timothy, *Irish Regiments in the Great War: Discipline and Morale*, Manchester: Manchester University Press, 2006

Boyne, Seán, *Emmet Dalton: Somme Soldier, Irish General, Film Pioneer*, Dublin: Merrion Press, 2014

Brennan-Whitmore, W. J., *Dublin Burning: The Easter Rising from Behind the Barricades*, Dublin: Gill & Macmillan, 2013

— *With the Irish in Frongoch*, Cork: Mercier Press, 2013

Brunicardi, Daire, *Haulbowline: The Naval Base and Ships of Cork Harbour*, Dublin: The History Press, 2012

Bunbury, Turtle, *Dublin Docklands: An Urban Voyage*, Dublin: Montague, 2009

— *The Glorious Madness: Tales of the Irish and the Great War*, Dublin: Gill & Macmillan, 2014

Bunbury, Turtle and Art Kavanagh, *The Landed Gentry and Aristocracy of County Kildare*, Dublin: Irish Family Names, 2004

— *The Landed Gentry and Aristocracy of County Wicklow*, Dublin: Irish Family Names, 2005

Burke, Tom, 'In Memory of Lieutenant Tom Kettle, "B" Company, 9th Royal Dublin Fusiliers', *Dublin Historical Record, Old Dublin Society*, 57 (2) (2004)

Caulfield, Max, *The Easter Rebellion*, 2nd edn, Dublin: Gill & Macmillan, 2014

Clare, Anne, *Unlikely Rebels: The Gifford Girls*, Cork: Mercier Press, 2011

Clark, Chris, *The Sleepwalkers: How Europe Went to War in 1914*, London: Allen Lane, 2012

Clarke, Kathleen, *Kathleen Clarke: Revolutionary Woman*, ed. Helen Litton, Dublin: The O'Brien Press, 2008

Collins, Jude (ed.), *Whose Past Is It Anyway? The Ulster Covenant, the Easter Rising and the Battle of the Somme*, Dublin: The History Press, 2012

Collins, Lorcan, *16 Lives: James Connolly*, Dublin: The O'Brien Press, 2013

Collins, Lorcan and Conor Kostick, *The Easter Rising*, Dublin: The O'Brien Press, 2000

Collins, Michael, *The Path to Freedom*, Cork: Mercier Press, 2012

Conlon, Lil, *Cumann na mBan and the Women of Ireland 1913–25*, Kilkenny: Kilkenny People, 1969

Coxhead, Elizabeth, *Daughters of Erin: Five Women of the Irish Renaissance*, London: Secker & Warburg, 1965

Cronin, Sean, *The McGarrity Papers*, Tralee: Anvil Books, 1972

— *Frank Ryan: The Search for the Republic*, Dublin: Repsol Publishing, 1980

Crowley, Brian, 'The Strange Thing I Am: His Father's Son', *History Ireland*, 14 (2) (2006)

— *Patrick Pearse: A Life in Pictures*, Cork: Mercier Press, 2013

Curry, James, *Artist of the Revolution: The Cartoons of Ernest Kavanagh (1884–1916)*, Cork: Mercier Press, 2012

Curtis, Maurice, *The Liberties: A History*, Dublin: The History Press, 2013

Dalton, Charles, *With the Dublin Brigade: Espionage and Assassination with Michael Collins' Intelligence Unit*, Cork: Mercier Press, 2014

Doherty, Gabriel and Dermot Keogh, *Michael Collins and the Making of the Irish State*, Cork: Mercier Press, 2006

— *1916: The Long Revolution*, Cork: Mercier Press, 2007

Dorney, John, *Peace after the Final Battle: The Story of the Irish Revolution, 1912–24*, Dublin: New Island Books, 2014

Doyle, Johnny, 'Major George Robert Playfair MC', available at http://johnny-doyle.blogspot.ie/2013/03/major-george-robert-playfair-mc.html (accessed 17 January 2015)

Doyle, Tom, *The Civil War in Kerry*, Cork: Mercier Press, 2008

Duffy, Joe, 'Children of the Revolution', *History Ireland*, 21 (3) (2013)

Dungan, Myles, *They Shall Grow Not Old? Irish Soldiers and the Great War*, Dublin: Four Courts Press, 1997

Dunne, Declan, *Peter's Key: Peter deLoughry and the Fight for Irish Independence*, Cork: Mercier Press, 2012

Dwyer, T. Ryle, *The Man Who Won the War*, Cork: Mercier Press, 2009

Elborn, Geoffrey, *Francis Stuart: A Life*, Dublin: Raven Arts Press, 1990

Ellman, Richard (ed.), *Letters of James Joyce*, vol. II, New York: Viking, 1966

Fallon, Donal, *The Pillar: The Life and Afterlife of the Nelson Pillar*, Dublin: New Island, 2014

Fallon, Las, *Dublin Fire Brigade and the Irish Revolution*, Dublin: South Dublin Libraries, 2012

Fanning, Ronan, *Fatal Path*, London: Faber & Faber, 2013

Feeney, Brian, *16 Lives: Seán MacDiarmada*, Dublin: The O'Brien Press, 2014

Ferguson, Stephen, *Letters, Lives and Liberty*, Dublin: An Post, 2011

— *GPO Staff in 1916: Business as Usual*, Cork: Mercier Press, 2012

— *The GPO: 200 Years of History*, Cork: Mercier Press, 2014

Ferriter, Diarmuid, 'In Such Deadly Earnest', *The Dublin Review*, 12 (2003)

Findlater, Alex, *Findlaters: The Story of a Dublin Merchant Family, 1774–2001*, Dublin: A&A Farmar, 2013. Available at www.findlaters.com (accessed 17 January 2015)

FitzGerald, Desmond, *Desmond's Rising: Memoirs 1913 to Easter 1916*, Dublin: Liberties Press, 2006

Foster, R. E., *Vivid Faces: The Revolutionary Generation in Ireland, 1890–1923*, London: Allen Lane, 2014

Fox, R. M., *History of the Irish Citizen Army*, Dublin: James Duffy & Co., 1943

Foy, Michael and Brian Barton, *The Easter Rising*, Stroud: Sutton Publishing, 2004

Gillis, Liz, *Revolution in Dublin: A Photographic History, 1913–23*, Cork: Mercier Press, 2013

— *Women of the Irish Revolution*, Cork: Mercier Press, 2014

Gonne, Maud, *The Gonne–Yeats Letters, 1893–1938*, Syracuse, NY: Syracuse University Press, 1994

Good, Joe, *Enchanted by Dreams: The Journal of a Revolutionary*, Dingle: Brandon Books, 1996

Goodman, Jordan, *The Devil and Mr Casement: One Man's Struggle for Human Rights in South America's Heart of Darkness*, London: Verso, 2010

Hastedt, Glenn P., *Spies, Wiretaps, and Secret Operations: An Encyclopedia of American Espionage*, 2 vols, Santa Barbara, CA: ABC-CLIO, 2011

Hay, Marnie, 'The Foundation and Development of Na Fianna Éireann, 1909–16', *Irish Historical Studies*, 36 (141) (2008): 53–71

— *Bulmer Hobson and the Nationalist Movement in Twentieth-Century Ireland*, Manchester: Manchester University Press, 2009

Hegarty, Shane and Fintan O'Toole, *The Irish Times Book of the 1916 Rising*, Dublin: Gill & Macmillan, 2006

Henry, William, *Supreme Sacrifice: The Story of Éamonn Ceannt*, Cork: Mercier Press, 2005

Herlihy, Jim, *The Dublin Metropolitan Police: A Short History and Genealogical Guide*, Dublin: Four Courts Press, 2001

Horgan, Tim, *Dying for the Cause: Kerry's Republican Dead*, Cork: Mercier Press, 2015

Jeffery, Keith, *Ireland and the Great War*, Cambridge: Cambridge University Press, 2000

Joye, Lar, 'TSS *Helga II*', *History Ireland*, 18 (2) (2010)

Keane, Elizabeth, *Seán MacBride, a Life: From IRA Revolutionary to International Statesman*, Dublin: Gill & Macmillan, 2007

Kelly, Brendan, *Ada English: Patriot and Psychiatrist*, Sallins: Irish Academic Press, 2014

Kelly, M. J., *The Fenian Ideal and Irish Nationalism, 1882–1916*, Woodbridge: Boydell & Brewer, 2006

Kenna, Shane, *16 Lives: Thomas MacDonagh*, Dublin: The O'Brien Press, 2014

Kennerk, Barry, *Moore Street: The Story of Dublin's Market District*, Cork: Mercier Press, 2012

Keohane, Leo, *Captain Jack White: Imperialism, Anarchism and the Irish Citizen Army*, Dublin: Merrion Press, 2014

Kettle, T. M. and Mary Kettle (eds), *The Ways of War*, Dublin: Talbot Press, 1917

Kiberd, Declan, *1916 Rebellion Handbook*, Dublin: Mourne River Press, 1998

Kostick, Conor, *16 Lives: Michael O'Hanrahan*, Dublin: The O'Brien Press, 2015

Krause, David (ed.), *The Letters of Sean O'Casey: 1942–54*, London: Macmillan, 1975

Laffan, Michael, *Judging W. T. Cosgrave*, Dublin: Royal Irish Academy Press, 2014

Lee, J. J. (ed.), *Kerry's Fighting Story 1916–21: Told by the Men Who Made It*, Cork: Mercier Press, 2009

Litton, Helen, *16 Lives: Edward Daly*, Dublin: The O'Brien Press, 2013

— *16 Lives: Thomas Clarke*, Dublin: The O'Brien Press, 2014

Lloyd George, David, *War Memoirs*, vol. I, London: Odhams, 1924

Loder, John, *Hollywood Hussar: The Life and Times of John Loder*, Wimbledon: Howard Baker, 1977

Londraville, Richard and Jane Londraville, *Too Long a Sacrifice: The Letters of Maud Gonne and John Quinn*, Selinsgrove, PA: Susquehanna University Press, 1999

Lynch, Diarmuid, *The I.R.B. and the 1916 Insurrection: A Record of the Preparations for the Rising, with Comments on Published Works Relating Thereto, and a Report on Operations in the G.P.O. Garrison Area during Easter Week, 1916*, ed. Florence O'Donoghue, Cork: Mercier Press, 1957

Lynd, Robert, *Galway of the Races*, Dublin: Lilliput Press, 1990

Lyons, F. S. L., *Ireland since the Famine*, London: Fontana, 1973

Lyons, J. B., *The Enigma of Tom Kettle: Irish Patriot, Essayist, Poet, British Soldier*, Dublin: Glendale Press, 1983

Mac Curtain, Fionnuala, *Remember … It's for Ireland: A Family Memoir of Tomás Mac Curtáin*, Cork: Mercier Press, 2006

Mac Lochlain, Piaras F., *Last Words: Letters and Statements of the Leaders Executed after the Rising at Easter, 1916*, Dublin: Kilmainham Gaol Restoration Society, 1971

Martin, F. X., *The Howth Gun-Running and the Kilcoole Gun-Running: Recollections and Documents*, Sallins: Irish Academic Press, 2014

Massie, Robert K., *Castles of Steel*, New York: Random House, 2003

Matthews, Ann, *Renegades: Irish Republican Women, 1900–1922*, Cork: Mercier Press, 2010

— *Dissidents: Irish Republican Women, 1923–41*, Cork: Mercier Press, 2012

— *The Irish Citizen Army*, Cork: Mercier Press, 2014

McCoole, Sinéad, *No Ordinary Women: Irish Female Activists in the Revolutionary Years 1900–1923*, Dublin: The O'Brien Press, 2008

— *Easter Widows*, New York: Random House, 2014

McElligott, Jason, 'In the Line of Fire', *History Ireland*, 20 (3) (2012)

McGarry, Fearghal, *The Rising: Easter 1916*, Oxford: Oxford University Press, 2010

— *Rebels: Voices from the Easter Rising*, London: Penguin, 2011

McGee, Owen, *The IRB: The Irish Republican Brotherhood from the Land League to Sinn Féin*, Dublin: Four Courts Press, 2005

McGlynn, Pat, *Éirí Amach na Cásca/The Easter Rising 1916*, Dublin: Republican Publications, 1986

McGough, Eileen, *Diarmuid Lynch: A Forgotten Irish Patriot*, Cork: Mercier Press, 2013

McKenna, Joseph, *Guerrilla Warfare in the Irish War of Independence, 1919–21*, Jefferson, NC: McFarland, 2011

McLaughlin, Robert, *Irish Canadian Conflict and the Struggle for Irish Independence, 1912–25*, Toronto: University of Toronto Press, 2013

McMahon, Paul, *British Spies and Irish Rebels: British Intelligence and Ireland, 1916–45*, Woodbridge: Boydell Press, 2008

McMahon, Sean, *Rebel Ireland: Easter Rising to Civil War*, Cork: Mercier Press, 2001

McNamara, Maedhbh and Paschal Mooney, *Women in Parliament: Ireland, 1918–2000*, Dublin: Wolfhound Press, 2000

Meagher, Meredith and Conor McNamara, *Easter 1916: A Research Guide*, Dublin: Four Courts Press, 2015

Mikhail, E. H. (ed.), *The Abbey Theatre: Interviews and Recollections*, Lanham, MD: Rowman & Littlefield, 1988

Mitchell, Angus, *Sir Roger Casement's Heart of Darkness: The 1911 Documents*, Dublin: Irish Manuscripts Commission, 2003

— *16 Lives: Roger Casement*, Dublin: The O'Brien Press, 2013

Monteith Lynch, Florence, *The Mystery Man of Banna Strand: The Life and Death of Captain Robert Monteith*, New York: Vantage Press, 1959

Moody, T. W. and F. X. Martin (eds), *The Course of Irish History*, rev. edn, Cork: Mercier Press, 2012

Morrison, George, *Revolutionary Ireland: A Photographic Record*, Dublin: Gill & Macmillan, 2013

Morrissey, Thomas J., *William O'Brien, 1881–1968: Socialist Republican, Dáil Deputy, Editor, and Trade Union Leader*, Dublin: Four Courts Press, 2007

Nevin, Donal, *James Connolly, a Full Life: A Biography of Ireland's Renowned Trade Unionist and Leader of the 1916 Easter Rising*, Dublin: Gill & Macmillan, 2006

O'Beirne Ranelagh, John, *A Short History of Ireland*, 3rd edn, Cambridge: Cambridge University Press, 2012

O'Brien, Paul, *Blood on the Streets: 1916 and the Battle for Mount Street Bridge*, Cork: Mercier Press, 2008

— *Uncommon Valour: 1916 and the Battle for the South Dublin Union*, Cork: Mercier Press, 2010

— *Crossfire: The Battle of the Four Courts, 1916*, Dublin: New Island, 2012

— *Shootout: The Battle for St Stephen's Green, 1916*, Dublin: New Island, 2013

Ó Bróin, León, *Protestant Nationalists in Revolutionary Ireland: The Stopford Connection*, Dublin: Gill & Macmillan, 1985

O'Callaghan, John, *16 Lives: Con Colbert*, Dublin: The O'Brien Press, 2015

O'Casey, Sean, *The Story of the Citizen Army*, Dublin: Maunsel & Co., 1919

Ó Comhraí, Cormac, *Revolution in Connacht: A Photographic History, 1913–23*, Cork: Mercier Press, 2013

— *Ireland and the First World War: A Photographic History*, Cork: Mercier Press, 2014

O'Donnell, Ruan, *Limerick's Fighting Story, 1916–21: Told by the Men Who Made It*, Cork: Mercier Press, 2009

Ó Duibhir, Liam, *The Donegal Awakening: Donegal and the War of Independence*, Cork: Mercier Press, 2009

Ó Duibhir, Liam, *Prisoners of War: Ballykinlar Internment Camp 1920–1921*, Cork: Mercier Press, 2013

O'Farrell, Mick, *A Walk through Rebel Dublin*, Cork: Mercier Press, 1994

— *50 Things You Didn't Know about 1916*, Cork: Mercier Press, 2009

— *1916: What the People Saw*, Cork: Mercier Press, 2013

— *The 1916 Diaries of an Irish Rebel and a British Soldier*, Cork: Mercier Press, 2014

O'Hegarty, P. S., *A Short Memoir of Terence MacSwiney*, Dublin: Talbot Press, 1922

O'Leary, John, *Recollections of Fenians and Fenianism*, 2 vols, London: Downey & Co., 1896

O'Mahony, Seán, *Frongoch: University of Revolution*, Killiney: FDR Teoranta, 1987

O'Malley, Ernie, *On Another Man's Wound: Personal History of Ireland's War of Independence*, Lanham, MD: Rowman & Littlefield, 2001

— *The Men Will Talk to Me: Kerry Interviews*, Cork: Mercier Press, 2012

— *The Singing Flame*, rev. edn, Cork: Mercier Press, 2012

— *The Men Will Talk to Me: Galway Interviews*, Cork: Mercier Press, 2013

— *The Men Will Talk to Me: Mayo Interviews*, Cork: Mercier Press, 2014

O'Rahilly, Aodogán, *Winding the Clock: O'Rahilly and the 1916 Rising*, Dublin: Lilliput Press, 1991

Ó Ruairc, Pádraig Óg, *Blood on the Banner: The Republican Struggle in Clare*, Cork: Mercier Press, 2009

— *Revolution: A Photographic History of Revolutionary Ireland, 1913–23*, Cork: Mercier Press, 2011

— 'A Short History of the Hibernian Rifles 1912–16', available at www.theirishstory. com/2013/03/31/a-short-history-of-the-hibernian-rifles-1912–1916/#.Urx4YNJ dXTo (accessed 18 February 2015)

Parnell Kerr, S., *What the Irish Regiments Have Done: With a Diary of a Visit to the Front by John E. Redmond*, London: T. Fisher Irwin, 1916

Pearse, Patrick, *The Coming Revolution*, Cork: Mercier Press, 2011

Pennell, Catriona, *A Kingdom United: Popular Responses to the Outbreak of the First World War in Britain and Ireland*, Oxford: Oxford University Press, 2012

Piper, Leonard, *The Tragedy of Erskine Childers*, London: Continuum, 2006

Plowman, Matthew Erin, 'Irish Republicans and the Indo-German Conspiracy of World War I', *New Hibernia Review*, 7 (3) (2003): 81–105

Quigley, Patrick, *The Polish Irishman: The Life and Times of Count Casimir Markievicz*, Dublin: Liffey Press, 2012

Quinn, Anthony P., *Wigs and Guns: Irish Barristers in the Great War*, Dublin: Four Courts Press in association with the Irish Legal History Society, 2006

Ring, Jim, *Erskine Childers*, London: Faber & Faber, 2011

Robertson, Nora, *Crowned Harp*, Dublin: Allen Figgis, 1960

Ryan, Anne-Marie, *16 Dead Men: The Easter Rising Executions*, Cork: Mercier Press, 2014

Ryan, Desmond, *The Rising: The Complete Story of Easter Week 1916*, Dublin: Golden Eagle Books, 1966

Schreibman, Susan, 'When We Come Back from First Death: Thomas MacGreevy and the Great War', *Stand To*, January 1995

Sheehy-Skeffington, Francis and Hanna Sheehy-Skeffington, *A Forgotten Small Nationality: Ireland and the War*, New York: Donnelly Press, 1916

Sisson, Elaine, *Pearse's Patriots: St Enda's and the Cult of Boyhood*, Cork: Cork University Press, 2005

Somerville Large, Peter, *Irish Voices: An Informal History, 1916–66*, London: Pimlico, 2000

Steele, Karen Margaret, *Women, Press, and Politics during the Irish Revival*, New York: Syracuse University Press, 2007

Stephens, James, *The Insurrection in Dublin*, Dublin: Maunsel & Co., 1916

Tarpey, Marie V., 'Joseph McGarrity, Fighter for Irish Freedom', *Studia Hibernica*, 11 (1971): 164–80

Tierney, Michael, *Eoin MacNeill: Scholar and Man of Action, 1867–1945*, ed. F. X. Martin, Oxford: Clarendon Press, 1980

Toomey, Deirdre, 'Gonne, (Edith) Maud (1866–1953)', *Oxford Dictionary of National Biography*, Oxford: Oxford University Press, 2004

Townshend, Charles, *Easter 1916: The Irish Rebellion*, London: Penguin, 2006

Voris, Jacqueline Van, *Constance de Markievicz: In the Cause of Ireland*, Amherst, MA: University of Massachusetts Press, 1967

Walsh, Pat, *The Rise and Fall of Imperial Ireland: Redmondism in the Context of Britain's Conquest of South Africa and Its Great War on Germany, 1899–1916*, Belfast: Athol Books, 2003

White, Gerry and Brendan O'Shea, *Baptised in Blood: The Formation of the Cork Brigade of Irish Volunteers, 1913–16*, Cork: Mercier Press, 2005

Wrench, John Evelyn, *Struggles, 1914–20*, London: Ivor Nicholson & Watson, 1935

FILMS AND DOCUMENTARIES

1916 Seachtar na Cásca – They Gave Their Lives For Ireland (Abú Media, 2010)

1916: Seachtar Dearmadta – The Forgotten Seven (Abú Media, 2013)

Irish Destiny (dir. Isaac Eppel, 1926)

A Terrible Beauty (dir. Keith Farrell, Tile Films, 2013)

WEBSITES AND FORUMS

1916rising.ie

1916rising.com

bureauofmilitaryhistory.ie

cairogang.com

decadeofcentenaries.com

dublin-fusiliers.com

fiannaeireannhistory.wordpress.com

irishgreatwarsociety.com

irishtimes.com/culture/heritage/century

militaryarchives.ie

rte.ie/centuryireland

therising.ie

therisingdead.com

FACEBOOK GROUPS AND PAGES

1916 Easter Revolution in Colour

1916 Easter Rising Historical Society

Brian Hughes – Letters of 1916

Dublin 1916: Then and Now

East Wall History Group

Fianna Éireann

Granny's Attic SE

Irish Volunteers.org

CONSULTANT BODIES

Adams & Mealy's Auction Catalogue, *Independence*, 2006–11

Adams & Mealy's Auction Catalogue, *800 Years Irish Political, Literary & Military History*, 2012, 2013, 2014

Bureau of Military History, Dublin

Dublin City Library and Archive

Glasnevin Trust

Killorglin Archive Society

Military Archives, Dublin

National Archives, Kew, Surrey

National Graves Association

National Library of Ireland

For regular updates on Turtle Bunbury's projects, visit turtlebunbury.com or follow his Facebook page, Wistorical.

PHOTO CREDITS

For permission to reproduce photographs, the author and publisher gratefully acknowledge the following:

© Author's collection: 232 (*top*); © British Postal Archive: 147 (*bottom*), 150, 151; © Cork Museum: 72, 133; © Dublin City Library and Archive: 187; © Éamon Martin: 127; © Eamon Murphy: 212; © Glasnevin Trust: 88–89; © Ibar Carty: 258; © Irish Capuchin Provincial Archives, Dublin, Ireland: 10, 13, 16, 17, 43, 56–57, 66-67, 87, 131, 147 (*top*), 179, 180, 183, 184, 209, 214, 278–79, 281, 284, 287 (*top*), 290, 291, 292, 293, 296; © Courtesy of James Adam & Sons: 30, 116–17, 143, 156–57, 161, 175, 199, 203, 211, 224, 239, 248, 252–53, 282, 287 (*bottom*), 295; © James Hardiman Library Archives, NUI Galway: 148; © Kilmainham Gaol Museum: 48–49, 80–81, 90, 136, 138 (*top*), 155 (*bottom*), 185, 204, 219, 220, 230, 254–55; © Library of Congress: 101; © Marsh's Library: 100, 191; © Mercier Archive: 14, 19, 20–21, 22, 28, 32, 36–37, 40, 44, 50, 58, 65, 68, 70, 82, 94, 96, 97, 98, 99, 102, 104, 106, 108, 110, 111, 112, 118, 122–23, 135, 139, 141, 142, 144, 154, 159, 160, 166, 168–69, 170, 171, 178, 188, 192, 195, 197, 202, 207, 208, 228, 232 (*bottom*), 234 (*bottom*), 236, 237 (*bottom*), 240, 241, 245, 246–47, 251, 259, 261, 263, 264, 266, 268, 269, 276, 288, 294; © Michael Collins Powell: 25; © Mick O'Farrell: 182, 244; © National Archives of Ireland (NAI), Census 1911, Dublin, District Electoral Division 44/49, A 15 return for the household of Elizabeth Dunne: 119; © National Library of Ireland: 129, 164; © Pádraig Óg Ó Ruairc: 221 (*top*); © Pat Quigley: 221 (*bottom*); © P. H. Lynch: 234 (*top*); © RCPI and Loopline Film: 223; © Courtesy of the Royal College of Surgeons in Ireland: 76; © Royal Irish Academy: 152–53 © South Dublin County Council: 215; © St Andrew's Archives: 18; © Courtesy of the heirs of T. W. Murphy: 138 (*bottom*), 146, 155 (*top*), 210, 249, 250; © UCD Archives, de Valera Papers, courtesy of the UCD-OFM partnership: 237 (*top*).

INDEX